Missouri

The Show Me State

Missouri

The Show Me State

Robert F. Brown

CLAIRMONT PRESS
Selma, Alabama

ROBERT F. BROWN is a native of Kansas City and grew up in St. Charles County. He earned a bachelor's degree in history and communications from Southeast Missouri State University. He has worked in journalism since 1979, including at newspapers in Piedmont, Caruthersville, Jefferson City, and Centralia. He also has worked in public relations for the State of Missouri and currently works in public relations for the Episcopal Church in Missouri. He resides in St. Charles with his family. Missouri history is one of Brown's hobbies, and he previously collaborated on *Horizons of Missouri*, a predecessor to this textbook.

Editor in Chief: Ralph M. Holmes

Supervising Editor: Kathleen K. Conway

Associate Editor: Billie Holmes

Design: Robin McDonald

Photo Research: Robin McDonald, Marie Martin

Production: Photographics, Birmingham, Alabama

Maps: Lee Windham

ISBN: 1-56733-062-2   Printed in the U.S.A.

To the Student

You are a Missourian. You may not have been born in Missouri, or someday you may move away from Missouri. But for the rest of your life, some part of you will always be a Missourian. It is something you can point to with pride.

This textbook was written to help you learn why being a Missourian is something special. You will learn about the people who made it a great place to live and the events that shaped its history. You'll discover its natural beauty and rich resources. And you will realize the challenges Missouri faces.

No book can tell you everything about Missouri. A book is only a key that can help you unlock the gates to different paths to knowledge. It is up to you to use the key and to explore those different paths.

Above: Higgerson School, a 1930s one-room schoolhouse in New Madrid. Front cover: "View of St. Louis" by Henry Lewis, painted in 1848. Page i: Statue of Tom Sawyer and Huckleberry Finn in Hannibal. Pages ii-iii: Gateway Arch, St. Louis. Pages iv-v: Missouri State Capitol dome, Jefferson City. Back cover: Statue of settlers heading west, Penn Valley Park, Kansas City.

This 1946 coal-fired steam locomotive in Jackson is still hard at work. It pulls passenger cars on a 9-mile tourist excursion.

Table of Contents

Chapter 1   **Learning About Our State**..............................1

Chapter 2   **The Land of Missouri**....................................10

Chapter 3   **Early Missouri**..40

Chapter 4   **The State of Missouri**...................................66

Chapter 5   **Missouri After the Civil War**.......................100

Chapter 6   **A Changing Missouri**.................................122

Chapter 7   **Modern Missouri**......................................146

Chapter 8   **The Struggles for Freedom**.........................168

Chapter 9   **A Rich Missouri**...188

Chapter 10   **Government in Missouri**............................202

Chapter 11   **Show Me Missouri**.......................................216

Chapter 12   **Missouri's People**..238

Appendix A   **The Symbols of Missouri**.........................258

Appendix B   **The Counties of Missouri**........................259

Appendix C   **The Governors of Missouri**......................263

               Glossary..265

               Index...270

               Acknowledgments.......................................278

This is the first electric drill used at the Bonne Terre lead mine. The mine has the largest man-made caverns in the world. It is now a National Historic Site.

Chapter One

Learning About Our State

Who are you? What words would you use to tell someone else about yourself? You would probably begin by saying, "My name is. . . ." You might say, "I am a girl (or a boy)." As you describe yourself, would you say, "I am a Missourian"?

   Being a Missourian is part of who you are. Because your state is such an important part of your life, you need to learn as much about it as possible. This book will help you learn about Missouri—Missouri as it used to be and Missouri as it is today. Missouri is a special place with special people.

Remembering the Past

How do we know about something that happened before we were born? You probably enjoy hearing your parents or other relatives tell about things that they used to do, perhaps before they were married. And you really enjoy hearing them tell of the funny things you did when you were a baby! You might have a baby book in which your parents wrote things about you. You might even have videos, photographs, and other things from when you were a baby. All of these things help you learn about and remember things in your personal lives.

   But how do we learn about and remember things that happened in our state long before we were born? We do it in much the same way that we recall our personal histories.

At Fort Osage, guides tell what life was like at the fort. These two men are dressed as an army private and a camp clerk.

History is the story of people—who they were, when they lived, where they lived, what their lives were like, and so on. We learn the history of our state by studying the things people have left for us as reminders of what happened in their lives. People who find out about the past are **historians**. You will be a historian as you study this book!

Clues to the Past

There are many clues that have been left behind for us to study. Historians collect these clues and use them to write books that tell us about the past. What kinds of clues are there?

Artifacts

Artifacts are one kind of clue. **Artifacts** are the everyday things that people made and used. We have tools and pottery from ancient peoples that let us know how they did some of their work. From later times, we have some of the clothes people wore, the toys they played with, and other personal items.

Documents

Documents are another kind of clue. **Documents** are written records of things that people did. Documents include legal records, diaries, family records, letters, and newspapers.

Oral Histories

An oral history is one of the most interesting clues to the past. The word *oral* means "by mouth," so an **oral history** is one that has been told by one person to another person. When the second person puts that history down on paper, it becomes **written history**. Here is an example of an oral history. This is part of a story that was told to your author by a very nice lady.

My father moved to this country from Germany in 1887. His family had lived on a large farm, but in his new country his farm was very small. Instead of a nice, big house, he lived in a soddie—a house made of sod cut from the prairie. After his first harvest, he went back east and married a long-time friend and brought her back to the farm.

One example of artifacts from later times is this mill equipment that was used in the 1800s. You can see the equipment at Bollinger Mill State Historic Site in Burfordville.

ORAL HISTORY FORM

Historian (your name)_____

Date_____

Name of person being interviewed_____

1. Were you born in Missouri? If not, how old were you when you moved here?_____

2. Why did you or your family come to Missouri?_____

3. What Missouri town did you live in first?_____

4. What is your first memory of Missouri?_____

5. Tell me about your first house here._____

6. If you moved here as a child, what work did your parents do? If you moved here as an adult, what work did you do?_____

7. What kinds of chores did you do to help your family?_____

8. What kinds of things did your family do for entertainment?____

9. What do you remember about the schools in Missouri?_____

10. What changes have you seen in our town in your life here?____

Top: In 1860, the Pony Express had its headquarters in the Patee House, a very fine hotel in St. Joseph. Today it is a museum. **Above:** The exhibits in the Patee House Museum include the last locomotive and mail car of the Hannibal and St. Joseph Railroad.

There, on the prairie, they raised a family, including me. But by the time I came along in 1901, they had built a large house that my sister still lives in today. It was fun growing up on a farm, but it also was hard work. Every day we had chores to do. I would feed the chickens and gather the eggs, help feed the cows while they were milked, and then take the milk down into a cellar where it would stay cool. Some of the milk we made into butter by hand with a churn. During the school year, we had to do our chores before and after school.

My brothers worked in the fields, using teams of horses to pull the plow or threshing machine. They had to care for the horses and their harnesses.

We, of course, didn't have television. In the evening, we often would sew or read and sometimes practice on our piano. On Sundays after church, we would often have family gatherings, with aunts and uncles and cousins who lived on nearby farms traveling by wagon to our house.

From this short history, we can learn many things about what life was like in the early part of this century. (A **century** is a period of 100 years.) In this case, we are referring to the period from 1901 to 2000.

You can **interview** (ask questions of) an older person in your family, school, church, or neighborhood to learn what that person's life was like in the past. You can start with the questions on page 3. Then add questions of your own. Write out the questions you want to ask before you start talking with the person. You may use a tape recorder so that you will not forget any of the facts. Always ask permission to write or record what a person is telling you.

Museums and Historic Sites

Museums and historic sites are places where we can learn more about our state's past. **Museums** are places where items from the past are on display. These items might include documents, clothes, tools, furniture, houses, cars, wagons—anything that tells us something about the past. **Historic sites** are places where important events took place. There are many historic sites around Missouri. Sometimes these historic sites have been turned into state parks.

Learning About Missouri Today

How would you describe Missouri to someone from another state? The state's Division of Tourism invites visitors to come "Where the Rivers Run." We learn about our state as it is today by listening to what people say about it, by reading about it, and by making our own observations about it.

Media

A good way to learn about Missouri is through television and radio news, newspapers, and books written about Missouri. All of these are referred to as **media**. What is recorded through the media becomes our history.

You can record your own history by keeping a diary. A **diary** is your record of what happens to you every day. Fifty years from now a historian could read your diary and learn what life was like for a fourth grader in Missouri at the beginning of the twenty-first century.

Observations

We can learn a lot about our state from **observations**, looking carefully at what is around us. What do our houses look like? What things do we use every day? How do we get to

Arrow Rock was one of the starting points for the Santa Fe Trail. Many buildings in the town are part of the Arrow Rock State Historic Site. This is a photograph of the Old Tavern, which was built in 1834.

The State Flag and the State Seal

The state seal was designed in 1822. But it was not until 1913 that Missouri adopted its state flag. The state seal is in the middle of the flag.

Many flags have flown over Missouri during its history. It wasn't until 1913 that the state had a flag of its own. Our flag was designed by Marie Elizabeth Watkins Oliver, the wife of a state senator.

The flag is divided into three equal parts, with red on top, white in the center, and blue at the bottom. The colors were borrowed from other flags. The blue comes from the French flag and the red from the Spanish flag. These two flags flew over Missouri before it became part of the United States. The white is found in both the French and Spanish flags. And, of course, the red, white, and blue are in the American flag. In the center of the flag is the state seal.

The state seal is found not only on the state flag, but also on many state buildings and official state papers. If you visit the Capitol and walk beneath the dome, look down and you will see a large bronze seal set into the floor.

The state seal is filled with symbols, including 24 stars that tell us Missouri was the 24th state and grizzly bears that stand for bravery and strength. At the bottom of the seal are the Roman numbers for 1820—the year Missouri applied for statehood—and the state motto.

The motto can also be found carved in stone above the front doors of the Capitol. The motto, in Latin, is *Salus Populi Suprema Lex Esto*. In English, that means "The welfare of the people shall be the supreme law." In other words, our state's laws should make life better for Missourians.

school? How do the people in our town earn a living? What does the land around us look like?

Symbols

We can learn about Missouri by looking at the symbols for our state. A **symbol** is one thing that stands for another. When we see one of our state symbols, we should be able to tell something about our state.

The state flag is one symbol of our state. There is a special section in this chapter on the state flag. Read it to see what you can learn about our state. Then, each time you see the state flag, you will be reminded of the things you learned about it.

The state seal is another symbol of Missouri. You can look for the state seal on government buildings and papers. There is more information on the state seal in a special section in this chapter.

Missouri adopted a state song titled "The Missouri Waltz." The words were written by J. R. Shannon and the music was written by John V. Eppel. The song was written in 1914 but did not become popular until Harry S Truman, a Missourian, became president of the United States in 1945. It was named the state song in 1949.

Missouri even has a state insect—the honeybee! Bees are important to Missouri's economy. They not only produce honey but they also help farmers' crops and fruit trees grow.

You will find other symbols as you observe our state. Businesses, sports teams, and clubs are the kinds of groups that have symbols. The symbols tell you something about the people who use them.

Maps

We can also learn about our state by looking at its shape and its location. A map helps us do that. A **map** shows how a place looks. Look at the map of the United States on page 8. Find Missouri. From this map you can see the state's shape.

The honeybee is Missouri's state insect.

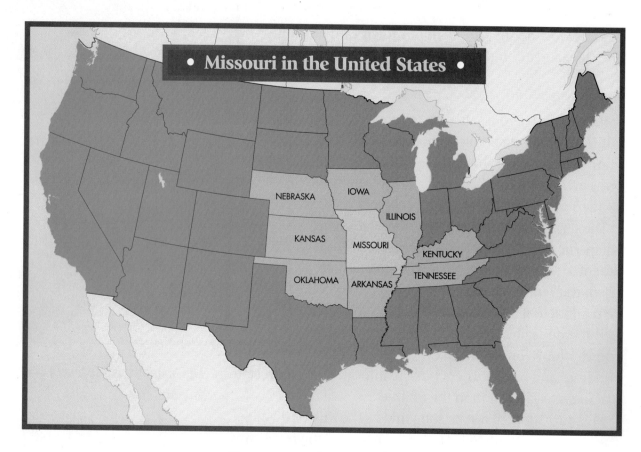

• Missouri in the United States •

NEBRASKA
IOWA
ILLINOIS
KANSAS
MISSOURI
KENTUCKY
OKLAHOMA
ARKANSAS
TENNESSEE

You can see the states that touch, or **border**, Missouri. You might even be able to see two long rivers that help make the shape of Missouri. You will learn about these things and many more in the next chapter.

Summary

In this chapter, you have learned that you are part of a special place called Missouri. Because you are a part of Missouri, it is important to learn about the state's past and the way the state is today.

You have found that you can learn about the state's past by looking at or studying artifacts, documents, oral histories, museums, and historic sites. You can learn about how the state is today by listening to people, by reading about the state, and by making your own observations. You learned about our state by observing some of the state symbols and a map.

Chapter • Review

Reviewing Vocabulary

artifact √
document √
historic site
media √
oral history

On a sheet of paper, write the numbers 1 to 5. Beside each number, write the word or phrase from the list above that best completes the sentence.

1. A bowl used by people who lived long ago is an _____.
2. Your birth certificate is one example of a _____.
3. _____ is the word we use when we speak of all newspapers, magazines, television, radio, and so on.
4. The first state Capitol in St. Charles is a _____.
5. One example of an _____ would be your grandparent telling you about his or her childhood.

Reviewing Facts

1. How do we learn history?
2. Name three things that give us clues to the past.
3. Name two places where we can learn more about our state's history.
4. Name at least three state symbols.
5. Name at least two things that a map can tell us about our state.

Using What You've Learned

1. Use the questions on the oral history form on page 3 to learn some interesting facts about a special person. Then share some of that person's history with your classmates.
2. Pretend that you have to teach a class about present-day Missouri. How would you find information to teach?
3. Design a symbol for Missouri today. This symbol must let people know something about present-day Missouri. Keep in mind what you would want a stranger to think about Missouri when you design your symbol.

Building Skills

1. Write a diary page about your day yesterday.
2. Use the oral history on pages 2-4 to answer these questions.
   A. The person telling the story got butter by
      1) going to the refrigerator.
      2) buying it from a store.
      3) using a churn to make it by hand.
   B. How do you think the person's father made his first house?
      1) Hired a carpenter to build it.
      2) Used stones he found in the creek.
      3) Stacked blocks of sod to make walls.

Did You Know?

- Arrow Rock was first named Philadelphia when it was settled in 1810. The name was changed in 1829.

Chapter Two

The Land of Missouri

What if you had to tell a visitor from outer space where you live? Where would you begin? Let us begin with the planet Earth.

Where Are We?

Earth is shaped like a **sphere**. That is, it is round like a ball. We can divide Earth into halves, or **hemispheres**, to make finding places easier. The **equator** is an imaginary dividing line that lies halfway between the North Pole and the South Pole. The part of Earth north of the equator is called the Northern Hemisphere. The part south of the equator is called the Southern Hemisphere.

Earth is also divided into eastern and western hemispheres by the prime meridian. The **prime meridian** is an imaginary line that runs from the North Pole through Greenwich, England, to the South Pole. The part of Earth west of the prime meridian is called the Western Hemisphere. The part east of the prime meridian is called the Eastern Hemisphere.

There are large bodies of land on Earth called **continents**. Missouri is on the continent of North America. North America lies in both the Northern Hemisphere and the Western Hemisphere.

On the continent of North America are **countries,** or nations. These countries include Canada, the United States of America, Mexico, and the nations of Central America. Missouri is a **state** within the United States of America.

Elephant Rock, near Graniteville, is a pink boulder that scientists believe is 1.2 billion years old. It weighs 680 tons.

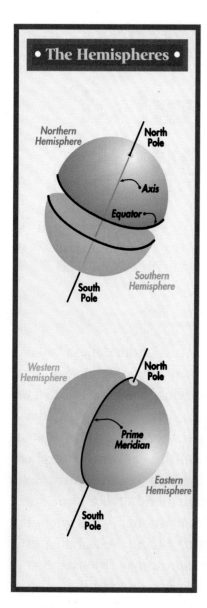

• The Hemispheres •

Northern Hemisphere

North Pole

Axis

Equator

Southern Hemisphere

South Pole

Western Hemisphere

North Pole

Prime Meridian

Eastern Hemisphere

South Pole

Within the United States, Missouri is one of the midwestern states. Look at the United States map on this page to find the other midwestern states. The eight states that border Missouri are Iowa, Illinois, Kentucky, Tennessee, Arkansas, Oklahoma, Kansas, and Nebraska.

Now that you have found Missouri in the United States, study its size and shape. Missouri is larger than most of the eastern states, but smaller than some of the western states.

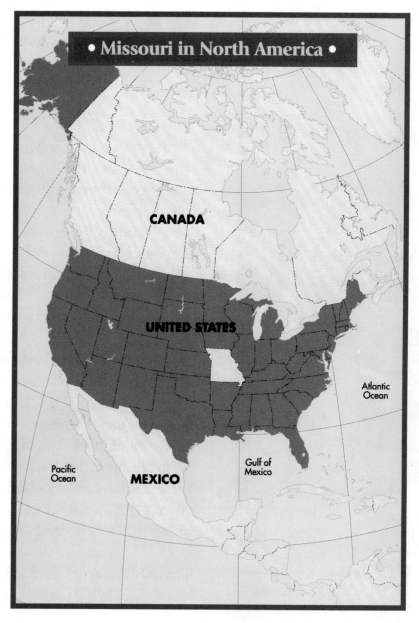

• Missouri in North America •

CANADA

UNITED STATES

Atlantic Ocean

Pacific Ocean

MEXICO

Gulf of Mexico

• Missouri Counties •

The shape of Missouri will be easy for you to remember. Some people say it looks like an old man with a beard. The part of Missouri that makes up the old man's beard is called "the Bootheel." Do you know why it is called that?

So far, you have looked at all the ways Earth can be divided to tell where Missouri is located. Missouri itself is divided into 114 parts called **counties**. Look at the map above and find your county. Or, if you live in the city of St. Louis, find St. Louis on the map, since it is not part of any county.

The Regions of Missouri

The words "from rolling rivers to rolling hills to rolling plains" can be used to describe the land of Missouri. Mighty rivers, hidden valleys, rocky hills, and fields that stretch to the horizon can all be found in Missouri.

Geography is the study of Earth—places and people on Earth and how they relate to one another. In this chapter and throughout this book, you will become a geographer! **Geographers** (people who study Earth and the places and people on it) often divide Earth into regions. A **region** is an area that has many common features. Geographers have divided Missouri into four regions based on the kind of land found there and how it was formed.

Missouri is divided into north and south by the Missouri River. We will begin our study of the different regions with the region to the north of the river.

The Missouri River, seen here near Rocheport, flows across the state from east to west.

The Glacial Plains

The Glacial Plains cover the northern part of the state from the Iowa border to the Missouri River. The **glaciers**, large sheets of ice, were one of the forces that shaped the landscape of Missouri. During the Ice Age, the glaciers stretched from the North Pole south to where the Missouri River is today. As Earth warmed up (about 500,000 years ago), the glaciers retreated, moving northward like huge bulldozers. In some places, they carved valleys. In other places, they crushed rocks into soil and left the land flat. The loose soil eventually blew into rolling hills.

Left: The North Fork of the Salt River is one of the many muddy, slow-moving rivers that flow through the Glacial Plains region.

In the Glacial Plains, the soil is very deep and good for farming. Because the land is fairly flat, the rivers run slowly, along paths that wind back and forth. The water is often brown because it is carrying so much soil.

At Long Branch State Park, the rolling grasslands have been restored. This vegetation is what early settlers might have found.

The Land of Missouri **17**

Above: This view of the Ozark Highlands region is from the top of Taum Sauk, the highest point in the state. **Opposite page:** *The rivers of the Ozark Highlands region are clear and swift. This is Mineral Fork, a river near Taum Sauk.*

The Ozark Highlands

Long before the Ice Age, Missouri was shaped by two other forces—volcanoes and an ocean. About 500 million years ago, much of the Midwest was covered by this ocean. We know this because of the layers of sedimentary rock found in the Ozark Highlands, a region that covers most of the southern and southeastern part of the state.

Sedimentary rock is formed when creatures living in the ocean die. Their skeletons sink to the bottom. Over millions of years, these skeletons form layers that are crushed together into rock. Often, you can see these layers when a highway cuts through a hillside. In some of these layers, you will find **fossils** (remains that have hardened into rock) of the sea creatures whose skeletons make up the rock. Some of this rock is easily dissolved by water and, over thousands of years, water seeping through these rocks has created caves. Missouri has so many caves that it is sometimes called "The Cave State."

When the water again reaches the surface, it comes out in springs. Some of these springs are very large, with millions of gallons of water gushing forth every day. There are more than 600 large springs in Missouri. Most of them are in the Ozark Highlands region.

But how did this region become dry land? Volcanoes beneath Earth's surface pushed up against the rock layers, raising them out of the sea. In some places, the hot, liquid rock (called *magma*) in the volcanoes broke through the surface and formed mountains.

In Missouri, these mountains are part of a chain called the Ozarks. That name is from the French abbreviation *aux arcs*, meaning "to the Arkansas" River. One of these mountains is Missouri's highest point, Taum Sauk Mountain in Iron County. Its **elevation**, or distance above sea level, is 1,772 feet. Taum Sauk was named by the Sauk Indians and may mean "big Sauk."

Missouri has thousands of springs that bring the underground water up to the surface. These waters from Maramec Spring, near St. James, flow into the Meramec River.

No one alive today knows for sure.

In this region, you will find **igneous rock**, rock that is formed when the magma cools. The igneous rock found in Missouri is some of the oldest in the world. It contains many minerals, including iron and lead ore. That is why there are so many mines in this region.

Because the land is so hilly and rocky, farming is very hard. Instead, the land is used for lumbering and recreation. The hills are not only pretty but also great for hiking and camping. The rocky stream bottoms keep the water clear and moving quickly, making it fun to canoe on the many rivers.

The New Madrid Earthquakes

This old engraving shows the damage caused by the New Madrid earthquakes. Many people feared for their lives and fled the area.

When we talk about earthquakes, we usually think about California or Japan. But did you know Missouri also has earthquakes and that the largest earthquake in North America may have happened here?

Earthquakes are caused when the plates that make up Earth's crust shift or bump into each other. The cracks and spaces between these plates are called *faults*. One such fault is the New Madrid Fault, which runs across southeast Missouri.

On December 16, 1811, the plates along the New Madrid Fault shifted near the village of New Madrid, a small town on the Mississippi River. The earth shook violently, so hard that church bells in South Carolina rang!

For two days the earth shook and the land rose and fell. In places, the ground split open and sand spit from the cracks. Some witnesses say the Mississippi River ran backwards. One family looked out after the earthquake to find that part of their farm was on the other side of the river.

Fortunately, few people lived in the area and there were few towns, so not many people were hurt or killed. When a second earthquake struck two months later, the few people remaining were scared away. It was years before settlers returned to the area.

The Southeast Lowlands

Just a couple of hours by car from Taum Sauk Mountain, the state's highest point, is Missouri's lowest point. It is near Cardwell in Dunklin County, where the St. Francis River crawls into Arkansas. It is only 230 feet above sea level. This area is part of the Southeast Lowlands, in the southeast corner of the state. This region includes the Bootheel.

The Southeast Lowlands were not pushed very high by the same volcanoes that formed the Ozarks. In fact, this area was

Left: The St. Francis River flows near Cardwell. The Southeast Lowlands has the lowest elevation in the state.

covered by water for a long time. Rivers flowing into the region deposited layers of soil. But much of the land was a swamp until the early 1900s. At that time, people drained the swamps to reach the trees that covered the region. When the trees had all been

In the Bootheel along the Little River in New Madrid County, the land is low and flat, and the rivers are slow moving.

harvested (cut down), the land was turned into farms. Today, it is one of the best **agricultural** (farming) regions in the state, growing wheat and soybeans and even cotton and rice.

The Western Plains

The southwestern third of Missouri is called the Western Plains. Like the Southeast Lowlands, this region was not pushed very high by the volcanoes that formed the Ozarks. Instead, the region remained very flat. It is part of the Great Plains, which stretch westward to the Rocky Mountains and northward into Canada.

In this region there are many large dairy and cattle farms. The cows graze on vast stretches of grassy pasture. There are also a number of mines in the southwestern part of the region, along the Kansas and Oklahoma borders.

Below: The grassy pastures of the Western Plains region are good for raising cattle. This cattle farm is in Barton County.
***Opposite page:** The 3,500-acre Prairie State Park near Liberal protects a variety of native prairie grasses and flowers.*

Storm clouds are gathering over these soybean fields in Mississippi County. Rain storms and thunderstorms are common in Missouri. But when we have too much rain, flooding occurs.

The Climate of Missouri

Visitors to Missouri who complain about the weather are told to wait, because "the weather will change in a minute or two." Of course, that is not really true. But the weather in Missouri can be hot like summer one day and cold like winter the next day.

When we talk about the day-to-day changes in the temperature or whether it is sunny or raining, we are talking about the **weather.** When we talk about the weather that occurs over a long period of time, we are talking about the **climate**.

Missouri's climate has four seasons. Spring arrives in March and lasts until June, when it gives way to the hot, humid days of summer. Fall arrives late in September and lasts until the first blasts of winter are felt in November. In the winter, the temperature can fall well below zero; in the summer, it often climbs above 100 degrees Fahrenheit. This type of climate is called *humid continental.*

Missouri's climate is influenced by four things: our distance from the equator, our distance from the oceans, our elevation, and winds. The farther from the equator a place is, the colder it usually is. That is why the temperature in Kirksville in northern Missouri is often 10 degrees cooler than the temperature in Joplin in southern Missouri.

Missouri is not near an ocean. But southerly winds blowing across the Gulf of Mexico often reach us, bringing warm, moist air. We do not have high mountains or their colder temperatures, but winds blowing from the mountains and Canada often reach us with their cold, dry air.

Sometimes, the warm, moist air from the south meets the cold, dry air from the north. Usually all that happens is that we get rain or snow, sometimes mixed with a little lightning and thunder. But the clash can cause **tornadoes**—violent windstorms that can knock down houses and pull trees up by the roots. That is why we have tornado drills in schools each spring, when the weather conditions are best for tornadoes.

Spring and fall are the two wettest times of the year in Missouri. An average of about 40 inches of **precipitation**—rain and snow—falls each year. In 1993, we had too much rain in the late spring and early summer. This caused the rivers in Missouri to flood fields and towns along the rivers. For many weeks, water covered large parts of Missouri. Many people had to leave their homes. It was one of the worst floods in the state's history.

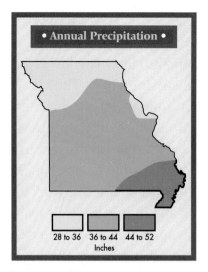

• Annual Precipitation •

28 to 36   36 to 44   44 to 52
Inches

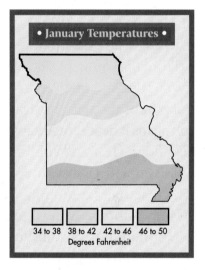

• January Temperatures •

34 to 38   38 to 42   42 to 46   46 to 50
Degrees Fahrenheit

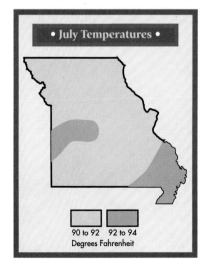

• July Temperatures •

90 to 92   92 to 94
Degrees Fahrenheit

Rivers and Lakes of Missouri

Missouri has many rivers that flow into either the Missouri or Mississippi rivers. The Mississippi River forms the state's eastern border, flowing from north to south. The Missouri River forms Missouri's northwest border. When it reaches Kansas City, the Missouri River turns east across the state to meet the Mississippi River north of St. Louis.

South of the Missouri River, on the northern side of the Ozarks, flow three long rivers. The Osage River begins in Kansas and flows slowly across the state to meet the Missouri River near Jefferson City. The Gasconade River twists back and forth across southwest Missouri to reach the Missouri River just west of Hermann. The Meramec River begins in the Ozarks and reaches the Mississippi River at St. Louis.

From the southern side of the Ozarks flow three more long rivers. The Current River flows quickly through the south-central part of the state, its clear, cold water rushing from many springs as it heads for Arkansas. Just to the east, the Black River also flows clear and cold into Arkansas before reaching the Mississippi River. Just a little farther east is the St. Francis River, which starts as a mountain stream but spreads out into a swamp before crawling into Arkansas.

North of the Missouri River, the rivers are slow, wandering streams with muddy banks and muddy water. In many places,

Left: From this overlook in Pike County, you can see the Mississippi River. The river forms Missouri's eastern border.

the rivers have been straightened by farmers to hurry them on their way. The Grand River flows out of southwest Iowa and enters the Missouri River near Brunswick, not too far from where the Chariton River joins the Missouri near Glasgow. The other

The spring-fed Meramec River flows through Meramec State Park near Sullivan. Visitors can rent canoes to enjoy the river.

Above: Prehistoric Indians held ceremonies along the banks of the Big River, seen here at Washington State Park. *Opposite page, above:* The Lake of the Ozarks was formed 65 years ago when Bagnell Dam was built. At the time it was the largest man-made lake in the world. *Opposite page, below:* This rock formation at Mark Twain Lake is called Buzzard's Roost.

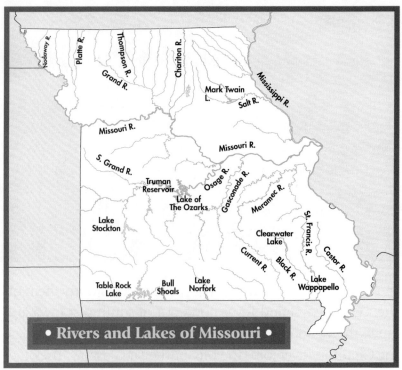

• Rivers and Lakes of Missouri •

long northern river is the Salt River, which crosses northeast Missouri before meeting the Mississippi River south of Hannibal.

Missouri also has a number of lakes. The larger ones were formed by dams on the major rivers. These dams were built to control flooding or to make electricity. The Osage River has two dams. Bagnell Dam near Camdenton forms the Lake of the Ozarks. Truman Dam near Warsaw forms Truman Reservoir.

A dam on the White River in Taney County forms Table Rock Lake along the Arkansas border. Other dams in Arkansas form lakes that reach into Missouri, such as Bull Shoals and Norfolk lakes. Stockton Lake was formed by a dam on the Sac River in Cedar and Dade counties.

A dam on the Black River near Piedmont formed Clearwater Lake, and one on the St. Francis River near Poplar Bluff formed Lake Wappapello. The newest of Missouri's large lakes is Mark Twain in Monroe and Shelby counties. It was formed by the Cannon Dam on the Salt River near Monroe City.

Plants of Missouri

Because Missouri has such a variety of weather and regions, it has a wide variety of plants. Scientists who study plants have counted more than 2,000 kinds of flowers, including the state flower, the hawthorn. Dandelions grow in our yards, and chicory grows along the roadsides. Rare orchids grow deep in the woods, and water lilies cover park ponds. There are other

Top: The passionflower is just one of the beautiful flowers that grows in Missouri. **Above:** *There are many pine forests in southern Missouri. These pine trees are at Hawn State Park.* **Right:** *Big Oak Tree State Park is home to many giant trees. This is the largest, or state champion, burr oak tree.*

plants, such as cottontails that grow in marshes. Prairie grasses grow as tall as a horse. Giant cane is made into fishing poles. And there are plants best left alone, like poison ivy.

When the first European explorers arrived, at least two-thirds of Missouri was covered by trees. Much of Missouri is still covered by trees. There are vast forests of pine trees in southern Missouri and tall cottonwoods along the rivers. The branches of giant oak trees spread as wide as a house. There are walnut, hickory, and pecan trees that give us nuts. Ash trees are made into baseball bats. Maple trees give us syrup and shade our lawns.

At Long Branch State Park, near Macon, you can see these native prairie grasses.

Animals of Missouri

The same reasons that give us such a wide variety of plants also give us a wide variety of animals. Around our houses we can find rabbits and squirrels. In the nearby woods, we can see deer, fox, and raccoon. At night, we might see an opossum, a skunk, or even a bat. Out on the prairie at night, we can hear coyotes howling.

Above us fly many types of birds, including the state bird — the eastern bluebird. We can see cardinals and blue jays, goldfinches, starlings, sparrows, and mourning doves at our bird feeders. In the woods, we can hear the knocking of woodpeckers. We might even see a turkey hiding in the underbrush.

We see geese and ducks along the rivers and at lakes and ponds. Out in the fields, we can hear the "drumming" of prairie chickens or the "bob white" call of quail. Many types of hawks and buzzards also fly high overhead.

Opposite page, above: The bald eagle, our national bird, can be seen in many parts of the state. Opposite page, below: Whitetail deer are a common sight in Missouri. Left: This box turtle was seen at Prairie State Park. Below: Monarch butterflies feed on fallen fruit at Arrow Rock State Historic Site.

Missouri has become a winter home for hundreds of bald eagles, which fly south from Alaska and Canada to find rivers that are not covered by ice. Some favorite places to find bald eagles are on the Osage River at Lake of the Ozarks and on the Mississippi River near Clarksville. Some of the eagles even stay in Missouri year-round and raise their young here.

The eagles are looking for fish, of which Missouri has many kinds. There are small minnows in creeks, and sunfish as big as your hand in farm ponds. There are bass as long as your arm in lakes, and muskies as big as canoes in some rivers. Catfish swim in both ponds and rivers. Some of the catfish grow as large as small pigs. A favorite fish of anglers is the trout. Many are grown in state-run trout farms before being turned loose in Ozark streams.

A sure sign of spring in Missouri is the sound of frogs and toads at night. And it is in spring that the box turtles try to cross the road to look for mates. Many types of lizards and skinks are found under rocks and in caves. Missouri also has several types of snakes. Most of them are harmless and even helpful, eating mice and rats that get into farmers' grain. Poisonous snakes can also be found in Missouri, but they generally avoid people.

And we must not forget all the insects in Missouri, from pesky houseflies, to busy bees, to beautiful butterflies and moths.

Earlier, you learned that geographers study not only the land but also the people on it. The people of Missouri are an important part of the picture of our state.

There are over 5 million people living in Missouri. That sounds like a lot compared to some of our western neighbors, but 5 million isn't a lot when compared to states east of us. In 1880, three-fourths of Missourians lived in **rural** areas (areas outside of cities). By 1930, less than half of Missourians lived in rural areas. Today, two-thirds of the population live in **urban** areas (towns and cities).

Missourians can trace their ancestors to many different people. **Ancestors** are those from whom we are descended —our parents, and grandparents, and great-grandparents, and so on. The first Missourians probably came from the west, not the east as later European settlers did. The first inhabitants of what we now call Missouri were prehistoric Indian tribes.

Above: This painting is of Haw-Che-Ke-Sugga, a Missouri chief. Opposite page, above: This man portrays a carpenter at Fort Osage, a living history museum. Opposite page, below: Missourian Thomas Hart Benton painted this mural at the State Capitol showing Huckleberry Finn and the runaway slave, Jim.

There were only a few Indian tribes in Missouri when the Europeans arrived in North America. Among the tribes who were here were the Missouri, from whom we get the name of our state. By 1840, the last of the Indian tribes had moved out of Missouri, forced out by the white settlers and the federal government. Many settled on **reservations,** areas of land set aside for the Indians, generally in the western states.

The first white settlers in Missouri were the French. They traveled along the rivers to hunt and trap animals for furs or to dig mines for lead. In 1803, the United States bought the territory containing Missouri from the French. After that time, large numbers of British settlers from the eastern states moved into Missouri.

Both the French and the British brought with them African slaves. A **slave** is a person who is considered to be the property of another and who is forced to work for that person. By the time Missouri became a state in 1821, one in every seven persons was a slave of African descent.

Midway through the nineteenth century, large numbers of German immigrants began arriving from Europe. An **immigrant** is one who comes into a country to settle there. The German immigrants had read stories about how much Missouri was like Germany. Until World War I, it was possible to find whole towns where very little English was spoken and where

the newspapers were in German. The Germans were soon followed by Italian, Irish, and Slavic immigrants.

Today's immigrants are more likely to be from southeast Asia, Mexico, and Central America. They come to Missouri for the same reason the first Indians did, the same reason the French did, and the same reason immigrants before them did—to find a better life.

Today about 89 percent of Missourians are white. Almost all the nonwhites are black, or African Americans. There are small but growing numbers of Filipinos, Asian Indians, Chinese, Koreans, Japanese, Vietnamese, and Latinos.

Missourians may also be grouped by their religion. Roman Catholics are the single largest religious group in Missouri, followed by the Southern Baptists. The majority of Missourians are Protestants. Nearly every **denomination** (religious group) can be found among Missourians, from denominations with churches in every town to denominations that have only a handful of followers.

The people of Missouri are also identified in other ways. In later chapters, you will learn more about the people of Missouri and how they use the land and its resources. You will learn that the land has shaped the people, and that the people have shaped the land.

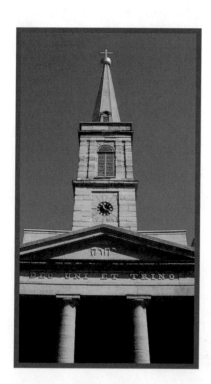

The Old Cathedral in St. Louis was built in 1831. It stands on the site of the first church built in the city.

Summary

In this chapter, you have learned the location of Missouri. You learned that it is in the western and northern hemispheres, on the continent of North America. It is in the midwestern part of the United States of America.

You learned that Missouri is divided into regions. These regions are the Glacial Plains, the Ozark Highlands, the Southern Lowlands, and the Western Plains.

Missouri's climate was described for you. You learned about the state's rivers. You also learned that Missouri has a wide range of plants and animals. Finally, you learned a little about the people of Missouri.

Chapter • Review

Reviewing Vocabulary

ancestors
continent
country
Ozark Mountains
precipitation
state

On a sheet of paper, write the numbers 1 to 5. Beside each number write the word or phrase from the list above that best completes the sentence.

1. South America is a _____.
2. Missouri is a _____ in the _____ of the United States of America.
3. Rain and snow are forms of _____.
4. The _____ were formed by volcanoes that raised the land up out of the sea.
5. Relatives who were born before us and our brothers and sisters are called _____.

Reviewing Facts

1. Name the imaginary line that divides Earth into southern and northern hemispheres. Name the imaginary line that divides Earth into eastern and western hemispheres.
2. What name is given to people who study Earth and the places and people on it?
3. Name the four regions of Missouri.
4. What is the difference between weather and climate?
5. Which rivers form part of the state of Missouri's borders?

6. One hundred years ago, did most Missourians live in urban areas or rural areas?
7. What is the largest religious denomination in Missouri today?

Using What You've Learned

1. Suppose the weather forecaster told you that warm, moist air was coming up from the Gulf of Mexico. Cool, dry air was coming down from Canada. The two were going to meet over Missouri. What kind of weather is possible?
2. Think about what you know about the Ozark Mountains. If you lived there, what would you do for fun? What could your parents do for work?

Building Skills

1. On a globe or map, find the equator and the prime meridian. Show a classmate the southern and northern hemispheres. Show that classmate the eastern and western hemispheres.
2. For one week at the same time every day, watch the birds around your house. Count the number you see. Make a chart to show how many birds you saw each day.

Did You Know?

- Elephant Rock is 27 feet tall, 35 feet long, and 17 feet wide.
- The highest waterfall in Missouri is Mina Sauk Falls in Iron County.

Chapter Three

Early Missouri

When did the first people come to what is now Missouri? And why? Why would people leave a place where they had lived, worked, and known other people to go to a place they had never seen? Why would people want to come to Missouri? Do people today have some of the same reasons for moving as our ancestors did?

The First People in Missouri

The first Missourians did not come from Europe, but probably from Asia. For some time after the Ice Age—as long as 40,000 years ago—scientists believe lower ocean levels left North America and Asia linked by a land bridge between Alaska and Russia. Today that area is covered by the waters of the Bering Strait. Many animals migrated across this land bridge, and so did the people who hunted the animals for the food and skins they provided.

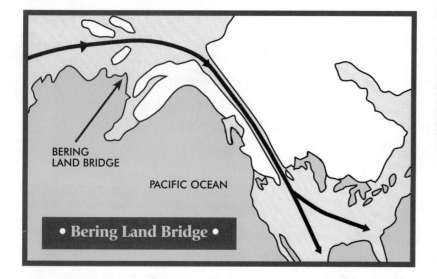

BERING
LAND BRIDGE

PACIFIC OCEAN

• Bering Land Bridge •

Above: At Graham Cave State Park, scientists found evidence that people lived in this rock shelter at least 10,000 years ago.

Using their stone-tipped weapons, the nomadic Indians killed mammoth and other large animals. Mammoth (large, hairy elephants) were native to the New World until about 6000 B.C.

These people settled in North America. Over thousands of years, their children and grandchildren and great-grandchildren and so on spread across the continent and into South America. Some of them settled along the Mississippi and Missouri rivers. We call these first Missourians **nomads** because they did not live in villages but followed the animal herds.

Some of the nomads began gathering nuts and berries. They discovered they could stay longer in one place and did not have to chase the herds. We call these people **hunter/gatherers** because they both hunted and gathered their food. They lived in caves and other natural shelters, such as the rock overhang at Graham Cave State Park in Montgomery County.

About 3,000 years ago, the prehistoric peoples we now call the Woodland Indians came to Missouri. These people knew how to make pottery from clay. In the clay jars they made, they were able to store food. They built simple shelters out of sticks and grasses and lived in small villages.

Gradually, the Woodland Indians learned more skills. They learned how to make tools and hunting weapons from rock and bone and how to grow their own food. Their villages grew into small towns. They learned how to farm from another group of prehistoric people known as the Hopewell. These Indians appeared in Missouri about the same time Christ was born.

The Hopewell were also traders, traveling far and wide to trade with other Indian groups. We know this because sea shells and rocks not native to Missouri were found buried in and around the mounds in their villages. The Hopewell built and used the mounds for religious ceremonies and as places to bury their dead. One of these mounds is found in Van Meter State Park in Saline County.

The Woodland and the Hopewell Indians disappeared about 1,000 years ago, conquered and taken to live with the

When the Woodland Indians began to grow their own food, they developed more permanent settlements.

*Above: The villages of the Mississippi Indians were often built around mounds as you can see. Often, there were also plazas where games were played. **Right:** These petroglyphs, or rock carvings, were made by the Mississippi Indians. You can see them at Washington State Park.*

Mississippi Indians. The Mississippi Indians traveled up and down the rivers trading with other groups of Indians. Their villages also were built around mounds. Many of their mounds were located where St. Louis is today. In fact, early settlers called St. Louis "Mound City."

The Mississippi Indians left many rock carvings of animals and strange creatures. Some of these can be seen in Washington State Park in Washington County. The Mississippi Indians also disappeared before the Europeans arrived. They were conquered by other tribes, some of which belonged to the Oneota and Quapaw families.

The Quapaw split into two groups. One group moved south to the Gulf of Mexico, the other moved north. The northern group was called *Wazhazhe*, or "the Upstream Peoples." This group included the Osage Indians, who were in Missouri when the Europeans arrived.

Towosahgy State Historic Site near East Prairie preserves the remains of an old Indian village. It was also a ceremonial center. This mound is one of five at the historic site.

Indians of the Historic Period

When the first Europeans came to North America in the late 1400s, they wrote about the land and the people they found here. Their written records have become our history, and we call the time of written records the **historic period**.

Christopher Columbus, a European explorer, was trying to find a new route to the Far East. When he reached America, he thought he had landed in India. He called the natives who greeted his boats *Indians*. Today, we use the word *Indian* to describe all of the native peoples who were here when the Europeans arrived. Some of these people prefer to be called *American Indians* or *Native Americans*.

Indians in Missouri

Very few Indian tribes were living in Missouri when Columbus and other early explorers arrived in America. A **tribe** is a group of people who have common ancestors and who share a name, language, and way of living. Many tribes hunted in Missouri, and most knew of "mighty rivers" in the lands toward the setting sun. As more and more Europeans arrived in America, tribes from the east were pushed westward into Missouri.

Scientists who study American Indians group tribes with similar languages into families. Indians who lived in Missouri were members of the Algonquian and Siouan families. Tribes belonging to the Algonquian family included the Sauk, the Fox, and the Illinois. Among the Siouan tribes were the Oto, the Iowa, the Quapaw, and the Kansa. The Osage and their cousins the Missouri also belonged to the Siouan family. It is easy to see where we get the names of many of our states.

The Missouri Indians were descended from the Winnebago tribe. Very little is known about the Missouri. They did not have a written language, and they disappeared shortly after the first European explorers arrived. It is known that they lived in

Charles Bird King painted this picture of chiefs of five Great Plains tribes—Oto, Kansa, Missouri, Omaha, and Pawnee.

• Indian Tribes in Missouri •

Very little is known about the Missouri tribe. But we do know that this is one of their arrowheads. It is on display at Van Meter State Park.

wigwams made from poles covered with reed mats. They used dogs to alert them to approaching enemies and to pull small sleds. When meat was scarce, the dogs became food.

It was the Osage who had the most contact with the early French explorers and settlers. The tribe lived along the Osage River in western Missouri. The name Osage is a French mis-pronunciation of *Wazhazhe*, the Quapaw word for the Osage. They called themselves *Ni-U-Kon-Skah* (pronounced "Knee You Con Skaw"), which meant "People of the Middle Waters." The Osage called the Osage River the *Wa-Tsi-Uzi* (pronounced "What See Oozy"), or "Snake with Mouth Open Waters."

How the American Indians Lived

Culture refers to the way of life of a group of people. It includes all of their beliefs, customs, activities, and possessions. The Europeans found it hard to understand the Indians' culture and said the Indians were "uncivilized." But that was not true—the Indians' culture was just different from the Europeans' culture.

Food

Like other tribes in Missouri, the Osage were mainly hunters. But they also were farmers who grew squash, **maize** (corn), and beans. The men would go out hunting in March, returning in time to plant crops in the spring. Setting out again, they traveled north to the Great Lakes and far out onto the Great Plains to hunt bison. They might walk or run as much as 60 miles a day. The men returned home in the autumn. Then they would harvest the crops before beginning another hunting season that lasted until winter. They stayed in their villages during the cold months of January and February.

There were, of course, no refrigerators in those days. The meat from the hunt was cut into strips, rubbed with salt, and hung from branches or poles to dry in the sun. This is very much like what we know today as beef jerky. The Osage were known for their generosity. Meat gathered on the hunts was divided so that the old, the sick, widows, and orphans had enough to eat.

The Osage and other tribes quickly adopted the horse when it was introduced by Europeans. The Osage became excellent riders. They used horses while hunting buffalo on the plains of western Missouri.

While the Osage men were hunting, the women stayed behind in the villages. They gathered nuts and berries and tended to the crops. They also wove baskets from grasses and turned animal skins into clothing using needles made from bones.

Shelter

Osage villages did not look like our towns of today. The Osage lived in circular lodges. Poles cut from trees formed the frame of the lodge. Reeds woven into mats made walls and roofs. Each lodge had a hole in the roof to allow smoke from the cooking fire to escape. Groups of seven lodges were located in the woods and along the riverbanks.

Government

Each Osage village was divided between two clans. The northern half of the village belonged to the *Tzi-Sho*, or Sky People. The southern half of the village belonged to the *Honga*, or Earth People. In the center of the village were two long, flat lodges built for the chiefs of each clan. The lodges were sometimes as much as 100 feet long. They were used for **councils**, or gatherings of the men of the tribe where important decisions were made. The lodges also were used for ceremonies.

Religion and Storytelling

Each day at dawn, the Osage would chant prayers to the sun, which they called "Grandfather." They also believed in *Wah-*

This 1804 painting is of Osage chief Le Soldat du Chene.

An Osage Wedding

When a young Osage man wanted to marry a young Osage woman, he would have his uncle tell her uncle. If her uncle agreed to the marriage, the young man's family would prepare a feast for the young woman's family. If the young woman's family liked the young man's family, they would show it by washing the food bowls after the feast. This was repeated the next day.

During both feasts, the family members exchanged many gifts. But the young man and the young woman were not allowed to see each other. They did not see each other until the wedding, on the fourth day.

At the wedding, the families exchanged more gifts. The young man then went to his lodge and waited for the sisters and aunts of the young woman to bring her to him in a buffalo robe. The young man would give the young woman a "burden strap" as a sign of respect. The woman used these straps to carry firewood and other bundles.

This painting shows Mo-Hon-Go, an Osage woman, with her child.

Kon-Tah, a "mystery force" that caused the sun, the wind, and the lightning and that controlled their lives. Fire was sacred and a symbol of "the spark of life." A sacred fire was always kept burning in the lodges of the chiefs.

The Osage often gathered to tell stories and recite poems, and this was a special time for them. The poems helped the Osage remember their history and customs.

Clothing

The Osage were unusually tall people. Many of the men were 6 feet tall. The French explorers wrote that they were great athletes. The Osage men shaved most of the hair from their heads. They kept a strip down the middle and attached turkey beards and deer tails to it.

The Osage traded for cloth with other tribes or European traders. They used berries and roots boiled in water to make dyes to color the cloth.

The Osage men dressed in blue or red breechcloths, deerskin leggings, and leather shoes called *moccasins*. They also wore buffalo robes when the weather was cold. The women wore moccasins and leggings with a blue or red

Artist George Catlin was fascinated by American Indians. He drew these young Osage warriors (above) and painted Tal-Lee, an Osage warrior of distinction (opposite page).

cloth around their waists and over one shoulder. Both men and women wore strands of beads and earrings.

When the French arrived in Missouri, there were about 7,000 Osage Indians. By 1825, however, the last of the Osage had moved out of Missouri to Kansas and Oklahoma. They were forced out by the government.

The French were the first to explore the area that would become Missouri. Pere Jacques Marquette and explorer Louis Jolliet traveled down the Mississippi River as far as the mouth of the Arkansas River.

European Explorers and Settlers

By the early 1600s, many European explorers had come to North America. Some of them traveled from Mexico across the Great Plains or up the Mississippi River. Most of them were searching for gold or other riches. As far as we know, none of them reached Missouri.

French explorers camping on the shores of the Great Lakes had heard Indian stories of great rivers to the west. The explorers thought the rivers might lead to the Pacific or the Atlantic ocean.

In 1673, a Catholic priest named Jacques Marquette and an explorer named Louis Jolliet led an expedition down the great river the Indians called "Father of Waters"—the Mississippi. An **expedition** is a journey for a specific purpose, such as exploration. The group went as far south as the Arkansas River near present-day Memphis, Tennessee. Along the way, they passed another great river that the Indians called *Pekitanoui* (pronounced

"Pea Key Tan Ooh We"). An Indian tribe living along its banks called the river the Missouri. Pere (the French word for *father*) Marquette described the Pekitanoui in his journal:

. . . sailing in clear and calm water, we heard the noise of rapids, into which we were about to run. I have seen nothing more dreadful. An accumulation of large and entire trees, branches, and floating islands were issuing from the mouth of the river.

Pere Marquette and Jolliet were the first known Europeans to set foot on Missouri soil.

Fur Trappers

Nine years later, the French claimed all of the land west of the Appalachian Mountains for France. They called it *Louisiana* in honor of the French king. It was not long before other Frenchmen, explorers, fur trappers, and missionaries began traveling down the Mississippi and up the Missouri. A **missionary** is one who is sent to do religious work in another country. In this case, the missionaries were hoping to convince the Indians to become Catholics.

The French built trading posts along the Mississippi. The trappers were called *coureurs de bois* (pronounced "Couriers Day Bwa"). The boatmen who traded along the rivers were called *voyageurs* (pronounced "Voya Joors"). The French were also looking for gold or silver. What they found were deposits of lead ore, an important metal used to make paint, glass, and bullets. The lead mines around Mine LaMotte, which were opened in 1715, became an important industry and remain so today.

In the 1600s and 1700s, fur hats and fur-trimmed clothing were very popular in Europe. The demand for furs brought French fur trappers to Missouri.

Fur trapping also was an important business. The French trapped or traded with the Indians for beaver, fox, otter, and other animal furs. The furs were sent back to France and made into fancy coats and hats.

In 1723, a Frenchman named Etienne Veniard de Bourgmont enlisted the help of the Missouri tribe to start Fort Orleans at the mouth of the Grand River, near present-day Brunswick. The fort made it easier for the voyageurs to trade with the Indians. But the fort was too expensive to run and only lasted six years. (The Missouri River has shifted its channel many times and wiped out all traces of Fort Orleans.) De Bourgmont returned to France, taking some of the Indian chiefs with him.

Early Settlers

The first permanent European settlement in present-day Missouri started around 1732. The farmers and lead miners at Fort Kaskaskia in Illinois crossed the Mississippi and founded the village of Ste. Genevieve. The first village site flooded too often, so the village was moved two miles west to where it is today.

The people in a French frontier village worked very hard in the mines and in the common field where crops were grown. But life was not all work. The villagers did find time for fun.

The Bolduc House in Ste. Genevieve, built in 1770, is an important restored Creole house. These views are of the back (left) and front (above) of the house.

Above: French houses were built with the logs facing up and down. Mud in the gaps kept out the cold. Below: This painting shows a battle during the French and Indian War.

The men spent their free time playing cards and other games. The women did not have as much free time. They were kept busy cooking, sewing, and caring for the children. But the women did find time for games and dancing. On Sundays, after the villagers had been to church, they held dances. Dances were also held on holidays and to celebrate just about anything.

The village houses were simple. Most were made of wood with thatch (straw or reed) roofs. The windows very often did not have glass but were covered with a cloth and shutters. Each house had a fireplace that was used for both heating and cooking. You can still visit some of these houses in Ste. Genevieve.

The main building in any village was the church. Each family contributed a part of its crops and other goods to maintain the church. The families also helped feed and house the missionary priest when he made his visits.

Spanish Control

Because France had claimed all the land west of the British colonies, few non-French settlers came to Louisiana. The Brit-

ish settlers stayed in their colonies along the Atlantic coast. The Spanish settlers stayed in the Spanish colonies in Mexico.

But events far from Louisiana brought changes to the territory. During the 1700s, France was often at war with Great Britain. One of their wars began in North America and was called the **French and Indian War**. France lost that war and had to give Great Britain its territories in Canada and those east of the Mississippi River.

Spain was an ally of France in the war. An **ally** is a person, group, or country that helps or cooperates with another. To pay its ally for the help, France signed a secret **treaty** (a formal agreement) with Spain in 1762 that gave Spain most of Louisiana. Spain mainly wanted the territory to keep Great Britain away from its gold and silver mines in Mexico. Overnight, the French settlers in Louisiana became subjects of the Spanish king. Because the treaty was a secret and because it took so long for news to travel in those days, it was two years before anyone in Louisiana heard about the change.

Meanwhile, many of the French who had settled east of the Mississippi moved across the river because they did not want to live in land controlled by Great Britain. Some of them decided to build a trading post where the Missouri and Mississippi rivers met. In charge of this adventure were Pierre Laclede, his wife Therese Chouteau, and their adopted son, 13-year-old Auguste Chouteau. Around Christmas 1763, they picked the site for the trading post and called it St. Louis. Laclede left young Auguste in charge of building the trading post while he was away in New Orleans on business. By the time word arrived that Louisiana was now a part of Spain, the trading post had grown into a busy little village.

Spain made very few changes in Louisiana. It did divide the territory into Upper and Lower Louisiana. St. Louis was the Spanish **capital** (seat of government) of Upper Louisiana.

Very few Spanish settlers moved into the territory. But Spain did welcome settlers from other countries as long as they were loyal to the Spanish king. Among the settlers was Daniel Boone, who was appointed a judge by the Spanish governor.

In 1763, Pierre Laclede (top) set out to find a place to build a new trading post. He chose a site near the mouth of the Missouri River. He left his stepson Auguste Chouteau (above) to supervise the building of the settlement. That French trading post became the city of St. Louis.

Becoming a Part of the United States

The Louisiana Purchase is remembered by this memorial on the grounds of the Missouri State Capitol. The statue shows the signing of the treaty by which the United States bought Louisiana from France.

In 1775, the **American Revolutionary War** began. The colonies wanted to be **independent** from Great Britain. That is, they wanted to be free from British rule. Great Britain asked several Indian tribes to help them keep control of the Mississippi River. On May 26, 1780, British redcoats (soldiers) and their Indian allies attacked the village of St. Louis. Luckily, the villagers had been warned. They were able to fight off the attackers. It was the only battle of the American Revolution fought in Missouri.

The Louisiana Purchase

After the United States gained its independence, more and more settlers moved westward. Many of them crossed the Mississippi River into the Louisiana territory. By 1800, there were about 10,000 white settlers in the territory. Most of the settlers were Americans. There also were about 1,000 African and Indian slaves.

Again, events far away meant changes for the territory. In 1800, Spain gave Louisiana back to France. This alarmed the United States, which sent representatives to France to work out a deal to protect American territory east of the Mississippi. To their surprise, France offered to sell Louisiana to the United States for $15 million. Louisiana—

which had been French, then Spanish, then French again—was now American.

The United States took control of Louisiana in elaborate ceremonies held in St. Louis on March 9-10, 1804. Spain had not yet had a chance to actually give Louisiana back to France. So, on the first day of the ceremonies, Spain transferred Louisiana to France. On the second day, France gave what was now called "the Louisiana Purchase" to the United States.

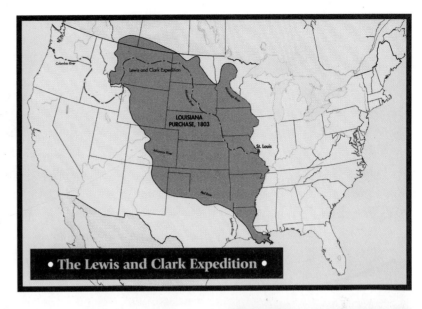

• The Lewis and Clark Expedition •

Lewis and Clark

Among the people in the crowd watching the ceremonies that March were Meriwether Lewis and William Clark. Even before the Louisiana Purchase, President Thomas Jefferson had asked Lewis and Clark to lead an expedition up the Missouri River.

The two men were in St. Louis preparing for what was called the "Voyage of Discovery." Clark and 43 other men left their camp near the mouth of the Missouri River on May 14, 1804. Lewis traveled by horse from St. Louis to St. Charles, where he met the rest of the group. They all left St. Charles on May 21. A large crowd cheered as they rowed their boats up the river. It was more than two years before they returned to St. Louis.

The group found that it was hard going against the river current. At times, they used long poles to push against the river bottom and move their boats upstream. Sometimes, men walked along the banks and pulled the boats by rope. By winter, the expedition had reached North Dakota.

While in North Dakota, the explorers met a French fur trapper named Toussaint Charbonneau. His wife was a Shoshone Indian named Sacajawea. Sacajawea served Lewis and Clark as an interpreter and guide through the mountains.

President Jefferson asked William Clark (above) and Meriwether Lewis to explore the vast territory that the United States had gotten from France. Their expedition left Missouri in May 1804.

The expedition eventually reached the **headwaters** (streams that flow from the source of a river) of the Missouri River in Montana. From there, the group traveled over the Rocky Mountains and down the Columbia River. They reached the Pacific Ocean in November 1805. They spent the second winter on the coast of present-day Oregon.

The voyagers turned around for home in the spring of 1806. When the expedition arrived in St. Louis on September 23, 1806, there was great rejoicing. The explorers brought back much information about the plants, the **geology** (the features and structure of the land), the animals, the mountains, the rivers, and the Indians along their route.

The Territory of Louisiana

The United States divided its new lands into two parts, the Territory of Orleans in the south and the District of Louisiana in the north. At first, the District of Louisiana, which included Missouri, was part of the Territory of Indiana. William Henry Harrison, a future president, was governor of Indiana Territory.

People living in the District of Louisiana complained that the governor was too far away in the territorial capital of Vincennes, Indiana. So, in 1805, Congress created the Territory of Louisiana. St. Louis was its capital. In 1812, the state of Louisiana entered the Union. The territory north of the new state was then renamed the Missouri Territory.

Trouble on the Frontier

As the settlers of the new territory established a government, new troubles with the Indian tribes began. The British caused much of the trouble. They hoped to use the American Indians to scare away the settlers and then claim Louisiana for themselves. At the same time, Great Britain and the United States were fighting the War of 1812.

To help stop the Indian attacks, now-Governor Meriwether Lewis had forts built along the Missouri and Mississippi rivers. The most famous of these were Fort Osage and Fort Howard.

*Opposite page, top: Sacajewea served as interpreter for Lewis and Clark. **Opposite page, bottom:** Meriwether Lewis and the others were gone for more than two years. **Below:** Fort Osage (left) was the second fort built in the Louisiana Purchase. The site was actually identified by Lewis and Clark.*

Fort Osage was built in 1808 along the Missouri River near the present-day town of Sibley (not too far from where Kansas City would one day be). Fort Howard was built on the Mississippi River near the present-day town of Winfield. It was abandoned during the war after nearby settlers fled to St. Louis. Fort Osage remained open after the war as an important training post. It finally closed in 1822.

In part because of the forts, the Indian attacks failed to scare away the settlers. The young American army and navy were able to defeat the British elsewhere. But it was several years before troubles with the Indians ended. It the meantime, the militia protected the settlers. A **militia** is an army made up of ordinary citizens.

This photograph shows the inside of Fort Osage. The officers' quarters are on the left. The fort was reconstructed using the original plans.

Summary

In this chapter you learned a lot about early Missouri. The prehistoric peoples were those who lived here before written records were kept. They arrived in what is now Missouri thousands of years ago.

The historic period began when European explorers started writing about what they found and saw. The early explorers were mostly French. They were soon followed by French fur traders and missionaries.

France established some settlements in the area they called Louisiana but later gave the territory to Spain. Spain gave the territory back to France just a few years before France sold it to the United States. We know that event as the Louisiana Purchase. Life in the newest American land was not easy. The settlers had to protect their homes and villages from Indian attacks.

Chapter • Review

Reviewing Vocabulary

capital
culture
expeditions
maize
tribe

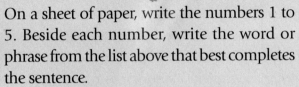

On a sheet of paper, write the numbers 1 to 5. Beside each number, write the word or phrase from the list above that best completes the sentence.

1. A group of Indians who have the same ancestors, speak the same language, and have the same way of life is called a _____.
2. St. Louis served as the _____ of Spanish Upper Louisiana and later of the United States's Territory of Louisiana.
3. Marquette and Jolliet and Lewis and Clark went on _____ to explore new lands.
4. _____ is a type of corn grown by prehistoric Indians in Missouri.
5. The way of life of a group of people is called their _____.

Reviewing Facts

1. How did the Indians use the mounds they built?
2. What is the "historic period"?
3. Why do some people call Indians "Native Americans"?
4. Name four Indian tribes that were living in Missouri when the early French explorers arrived.

5. Which European country sent explorers down the Mississippi River?
6. What is the name of the first permanent European settlement in Missouri?
7. From what country did the United States buy Louisiana?

Using What You've Learned

1. Read the description of an Osage village on page 50. Draw a picture of what you think the village looked like.
2. It is your job to tell early settlers what is most important for survival in Missouri. Make a list of the things you would tell them.

Building Skills

1. Imagine you are one of the first non-Indians to live in Missouri. What would you do to make friends with the Indians?
2. Choose one of the famous people mentioned in this chapter. How would you convince others that the person you have chosen was the most important person in Missouri's early history?
3. Pretend that you are an Indian boy or girl. Write a paragraph describing one day in your life.

Did You Know?

- The Osage Indians called the village of St. Louis "Chouteau's Town."
- Auguste Chouteau became an Osage blood brother.

Chapter Four

The State of Missouri

Above: *In 1820, Alexander McNair was elected the first governor of the state of Missouri.* **Opposite page:** *The first State Capitol was in St. Charles. The General Assembly met in the rooms on the second floor of this building. The building's owners lived on the first floor and operated a general store.*

When Missouri became part of the United States, the president and Congress appointed the territorial governor. The people of the territory did elect representatives to the territorial legislature. Still, many of the rules were made *for* the people and not *by* the people.

This was all right for a while in Missouri because there were few people in the territory. Missouri needed the United States to provide protection and other services. But more and more people were moving into Missouri. By 1820, the population had grown to 66,000 people, and 10,000 of those were slaves. The people felt more and more that they could govern themselves by becoming a state.

Statehood

In 1818, the territorial legislature asked Congress to consider statehood for Missouri. This caused a bitter debate in Congress. Congress considered Missouri a "slave state" because there were slaves already in Missouri. A **slave state** was one that permitted slavery; a **free state** was one that did not permit slavery.

The 11 northern states were all free states. They did not want to admit any more slave states into the Union or allow any more slaves into Missouri. The 11 southern states were all slave states. They were afraid that if there were more free states Congress would one day ban (forbid) all slavery.

The northern states said they would not admit Missouri as a slave state. The southern states said they would not admit Maine, a nonslave territory, as a state if Missouri could not enter

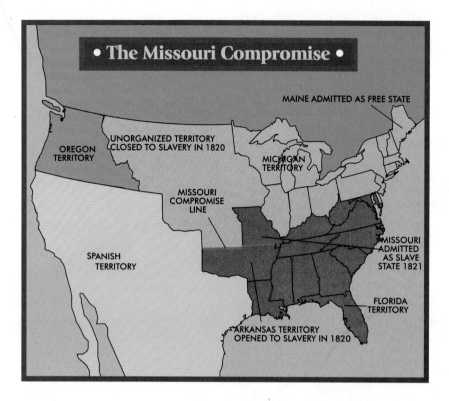

• The Missouri Compromise •

MAINE ADMITTED AS FREE STATE

OREGON TERRITORY

UNORGANIZED TERRITORY CLOSED TO SLAVERY IN 1820

MICHIGAN TERRITORY

MISSOURI COMPROMISE LINE

SPANISH TERRITORY

MISSOURI ADMITTED AS SLAVE STATE 1821

FLORIDA TERRITORY

ARKANSAS TERRITORY OPENED TO SLAVERY IN 1820

as a slave state. The argument was settled by the Missouri Compromise of 1820. In a **compromise**, each side gives way a little in its demands. The **Missouri Compromise** allowed Missouri to enter the Union as a slave state and Maine as a free state. But no more slave states would be allowed north of a line even with Missouri's southern border.

This compromise settled the question of Missouri's statehood. But it further divided the northern states from the southern states over slavery and states' rights. **States' rights** is the belief that the rights of a state are more important than the rights of the federal government. Many people see this division as the first step toward the Civil War.

In June 1820, representatives from all over Missouri met in St. Louis to write a constitution. A **constitution** is a document that sets out the rules under which a government will operate. This was the last step toward becoming a state. Congress approved the state constitution. Missouri was admitted to the Union as the 24th state on August 10, 1821.

Choosing a Capital

One of the first decisions the new legislature had to make was the location for the state capital. The new constitution required that the capital be built within a day's ride by horse from the mouth of the Osage River. That was to make sure the capital would be located in the center of the state. A group appointed by the legislature chose a high spot on the north side of the Osage

River in Callaway County as the site for the capital. But the land cost too much, so the group chose a second site on the south side of the river in Cole County. The capital was named Jefferson City after President Thomas Jefferson. The state government moved there in 1826 from the temporary capital of St. Charles.

This is a view of Jefferson City in the 1850s. The State Capitol is the large domed building in the upper left.

Making a Living

The **economy** is the whole system of growing, making, selling, buying, and using goods and services. To be successful, a state must have a strong economy. When Missouri became a state, fur trading was still its most important industry. But most Missourians were farmers, and the state had a growing agricultural economy.

Agriculture

The farmers in Missouri grew corn, wheat, or oats and raised cows, horses, and pigs. Much of Missouri was covered by trees, so the farmers first had to cut down the trees. Then they had to pull up the stumps and roots and clear away any rocks from the fields. A lot of this work was done by hand or with the help of oxen, horses, and mules. On larger farms, slaves cleared and worked in the fields.

Most of the farms were small, with a log cabin, a simple barn, and a few fields. The farms also had gardens where the family grew vegetables. Vegetables from the garden were either stored in a cool cellar dug into the earth below the cabin or dried and kept in jars.

Usually, the farm had a cow, which was milked twice a day. Thick cream rose to the top of the milk. The farmer's wife and

Left: Clearing land for farming was difficult and took a lot of time. Once a tree was cut down, the stump had to be removed. That might take a month!

children used a churn to turn the cream into butter. They kept the milk cool by putting it in a well filled with cold water or in a nearby cave.

The cows were allowed to graze in the clearings in the woods or on the hillsides. Pigs were either kept in pens or allowed to

Many German settlers came to Missouri. One place they settled was Frohna. You can see some of the cabins they built at Saxon Lutheran Memorial.

roam the woods to eat acorns and other nuts. If the farm had chickens, the children would gather eggs each morning. The farmer and his sons also hunted for meat and furs.

Much of what the farmer grew he kept for the use of his family and his animals. The grain was stored in bins to protect it from the weather, mice, and rats. Corn and wheat were taken to a mill. There they were ground into cornmeal or flour and put into sacks. If there was any grain left over, the farmer sold or traded it in a nearby town for things the family needed.

These photographs were taken at Missouri Town 1855, an outdoor museum near Blue Springs. The buildings there recreate a typical midwestern village of the 1850s.

In the southeast part of the state, a few farmers grew cotton as a **cash crop**, a crop that was raised to be sold for a profit. Along the Missouri River, some farmers grew tobacco. Other cash crops in Missouri were hemp, flax, barley, and grapes. Farmers also sold the left-over wood from the trees they cleared from their land.

This large house belonged to a well-to-do farmer. The building in the back is the summer kitchen. The farmer's barn is pictured on the opposite page.

Early Businesses

Of course, not all Missourians were farmers. There were still many fur trappers. In the villages, there were trading posts and other shops that sold goods needed by people on the frontier. (The **frontier** was the area just on the edge of a settled area.) In a village, there was usually a general store that sold a little

Left: "Interpreters" at Missouri Town dress in clothing of the 1850s and explain what life was like at that time. This man is portraying a black-smith. Others demonstrate the daily routines of villagers.

bit of everything. There would be all sorts of goods, cloth to make clothes, books, glass for windows, kitchen utensils, and other things that a frontier family needed but could not make themselves.

Also in the village, there was usually a blacksmith shop. The blacksmith turned iron into tools, nails, horseshoes, and other metal objects such as door hinges and wagon wheels. There

The Felix Valle House in Ste. Genevieve is a state historic site. Built in 1818, the house was both the home and the office for the Valle family.

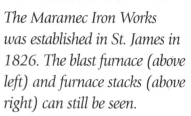

The Maramec Iron Works was established in St. James in 1826. The blast furnace (above left) and furnace stacks (above right) can still be seen.

might also be a cooper, a person who made barrels and buckets. A gunsmith made and repaired guns. There would be at least one livery stable, where horses were kept and where the harnesses used on the horses were made and repaired. There might also be a shop where newspapers and books were printed and sold.

Most of the goods sold in the general store were made in factories in the eastern states. Later, factories were built in Missouri. Shoe factories, meat-packing houses, flour mills, wagon makers, wool and cotton mills, and breweries were some of the early manufacturing businesses in Missouri.

Above and opposite page top: The Watkins Woolen Mill was built in 1861 near Excelsior Springs. This state historic site contains original machinery.

78   Missouri: *The Show Me State*

Getting Around Missouri

Before the settlers came to Missouri, the American Indians, explorers, and fur trappers traveled either by foot following trails through the woods or by canoe on the rivers. The settlers brought oxen, mules, and horses, with wagons. The trails grew into roads. The roads were usually just dirt, which turned to mud in the rain and snow. Sometimes the roads were paved with boards called *planks* or with stones or bricks. A ride on these early paved roads was very bumpy!

River Travel

To move all the goods being traded, larger boats replaced the canoes on the rivers. Wooden flatboats and keelboats moved along with the river current. A **flatboat** was a raft with sides. A **keelboat** had a bow and a keel, which was a strong piece of wood or metal that ran along the bottom of the boat. Both types of riverboats moved downstream with the help of men pushing poles against the river bottom. Sometimes when the boat reached its destination downstream, the cargo was unloaded and the boat taken apart. The riverboat men would then sell the wood and find a different way home.

Poles were also used to push the boats upstream, although that was much harder to do. Sometimes passengers walked along the riverbanks and pulled the boats with ropes. Some boats had sails to use when the wind was blowing just right. Going against the current was slow, often only 10 miles a day. It could take three months or more to go from New Orleans to St. Louis.

By the time Missouri became a state, boats driven by steam were seen along the Mississippi, Missouri, Gasconade, and Osage rivers. The first steamboat on the Mississippi, the *Zebulon M. Pike*, arrived in St. Louis in 1817. The first steamboat on the Missouri, the *Independence*, reached Franklin in 1819. Before long, steamboats crowded the riverfronts of towns up and down the rivers. Many of these towns, like Glasgow, Lexington, and Weston, grew into important river ports. A steamboat

In his painting "The Jolly Flatboatmen in Port," George Caleb Bingham depicts the happy end to a long journey.

Henry Lewis painted "View of St. Louis" in 1846. St. Louis was an important river port. It was not uncommon for more than 100 steamboats to be tied up along the riverfront.

arriving in a small town was a big event. The townspeople would rush to the riverfront when they heard the call "Ste-e-e-eamboat a comin'!"

The boats carried everything, including livestock (horses, cattle, sheep, and hogs) and people. Boats going up the Missouri and Osage rivers often carried settlers and wagons. Boats on the Mississippi were usually larger and fancier. But travel on a steamboat could be dangerous. The boat might hit a snag like a sunken tree and sink, run aground on a sandbar, or have its steam boiler explode.

Stagecoaches and Railroads

Steam power was used not only on the rivers but also in a new invention called a *locomotive*. The locomotive ran on iron rails and pulled cars carrying goods or people linked together in a train. Unlike the steamboats, the railroads did not have to depend on rivers and could go more places in shorter times.

But before there were railroads, wagons pulled by horses, oxen, or mules carried goods and people. Many eager traders and travelers started their journeys to the west from Missouri, following famous routes like the Santa Fe and Oregon trails.

The Santa Fe Trail led traders to the southwestern part of the United States and to Mexico. It originally started in Franklin, along the Missouri River. The starting place later moved to Arrow Rock, and later still to Independence. In some places along the old trail route, you can still see ruts left by the wagon wheels.

The Oregon Trail also started in Independence. Settlers traveled with all their belongings by steamboat up the Missouri River to Independence or St. Joseph. There, they bought covered wagons and supplies and joined a wagon train headed west to Oregon or California.

Another way to travel was by **stagecoach**, a large wagon that had a roof and that was pulled by several horses. The stagecoaches were an early version of buses. They ran set routes between towns carrying people and the mail. A trip on a stagecoach could be bumpy and dusty. In his book *Roughing It*, Mark Twain wrote about a stagecoach trip he took.

We began to get into country, now threaded here and there with little streams. These had high, steep banks on each side, and every time we flew down one bank and scrambled up the other, our party inside got mixed somewhat. First we would all be down in a pile in the forward end of the stage, nearly in a sitting posture, and in a second we would shoot to the other end, and stand on our heads.

The first stagecoach in Missouri traveled between St. Louis and Franklin in 1819. In 1858, John Butterfield and William Fargo started a stagecoach company. It took passengers and

• The Santa Fe and Oregon Trails •

• Railroads in 1860 •

1. Hannibal & St. Joseph Railroad
2. North Missouri Railroad
3. Pacific Railroad
4. Southwest Branch Pacific Railroad
5. Iron Mountain Railroad

mail from Tipton, through Springfield, into Arkansas, and on to San Francisco, California. Called the Overland Mail, the trip to California took 24 days and cost $200 in gold. But you could send a letter on the Overland Mail for just 20 cents.

The first railroad in Missouri was the Pacific Railroad, which started in St. Louis in 1852. By 1855, it had reached Jefferson City. But there was a disaster on its first trip to the capital. Many government and railroad officials were on that first train to Jefferson City. Railroad crews had worked quickly to finish a bridge over the Gasconade River east of the city. But the bridge was too weak to hold the weight of the train. The train crashed through the wooden timbers into the river, killing 31 people.

The part of the Pacific Railroad between St. Louis and Kansas City was not completed until 1865. But the Hannibal and St. Joseph Railroad crossed the state in 1859. It was not long after the Civil War that railroads reached most parts of Missouri.

Independence was the starting point for the Santa Fe and Oregon trails. In this painting, you can see the wagons lined up in Independence Square in front of the Jackson County Courthouse.

The railroads brought many people to the state. Some of them stopped along the rail lines to start towns like Moberly, Rolla, and Marceline. The railroad companies owned much of the land along their routes. They encouraged farmers from other states and other countries to come to Missouri and settle. The farmers' grain and livestock were then shipped on the railroads.

Some important riverboat towns, like St. Louis and Hannibal, became important railroad towns. Many riverboat towns, however, faded away as railroads replaced steamboats. The town that benefited the most from the arrival of the railroads was Kansas City. When the first railroad reached it in 1865, it had fewer than 5,000 people. Within ten years of the railroad's arrival, it had grown to more than 32,000 people.

Above left: This old engraving shows both a stagecoach traveling along a plank road (left) and an early railroad (right). Opposite page below: This Overland Mail stagecoach is getting ready for its regular trip between St. Louis and San Francisco. Above: The Martin Hotel in Versailles was a regular stop on the stagecoach line. Today it is the Morgan County Historical Museum.

The Pony Express

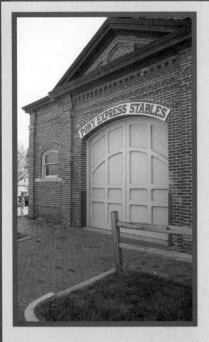

In 1859, posters appeared around St. Joseph advertising jobs for "small, wiry fellows," preferably orphans. The posters were for jobs as riders on the Pony Express. Small, fast ponies would be used to carry the mail from St. Joseph to Sacramento, California. That meant the riders had to be small. Every ounce of weight was important. The route across the Great Plains and through the Rocky Mountains was filled with danger from the weather, rattlesnakes, wolves, bears, robbers, and Indians. Orphans were preferred because it was thought they would be more willing to face the daily dangers.

The first riders left St. Joseph and Sacramento on April 3, 1860. Carrying mail in leather pouches, the riders went from one station to the next, a distance of about 20 miles. At the new station, the rider grabbed the mail pouches, jumped off one pony, and quickly jumped on another. When the rider tired, a new one took his place. The mail never stopped along its route.

Before the Pony Express, mail to and from California was carried by stagecoach. It took at least three weeks for a letter to travel from St. Louis to San Francisco. The Pony Express carried the letter to California in 11 days.

As exciting as it was, the Pony Express was a financial disaster for its investors. They did not have to suffer long, however. Just six months after the first riders completed their routes, the first telegraph line across the United States was completed. Messages could now be sent almost at once, putting the Pony Express out of business.

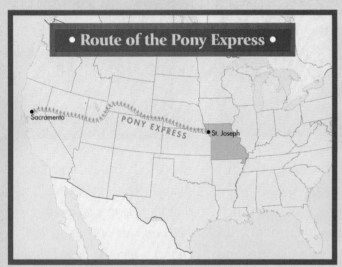

• Route of the Pony Express •

The red brick stable in St. Joseph where the Pony Express started is now a museum with exhibits on the beginning and end of that famous mail service.

Above: *This statue in St. Joseph honors the Pony Express riders who made the difficult 1,966-mile trip.* **Left:** *The office for the Pony Express has been recreated in the Patee House Museum.*

The Civil War

Just as the issues of slavery and states' rights were dividing the nation, they were also dividing Missouri.

Slavery

Missouri had known slavery from its earliest history. American Indian tribes in Missouri often made slaves of people from other tribes they captured in battle. But the Indians did not buy or sell people as slaves until they started trading with the European settlers.

The first African slaves were brought to Missouri by the French in 1720 to work in the lead and iron mines. By the time of the Louisiana Purchase in 1803, there were about 1,400 black slaves out of the population of 10,300 non-Indians in Missouri. When Missouri became a state in 1821, there were 10,000 black slaves out of a total population of 66,000. The majority of the slaves lived in the counties along the Missouri River, where most of the settlers from other slave states lived.

Slaves in Missouri did not live on large plantations as they did in the South. Instead they worked in small numbers on small farms. They plowed, planted, and harvested crops and took care of the livestock. Other slaves worked in the towns as servants or laborers. Slaves began working as soon as they were old enough to do chores. They worked from sunup to sundown every day except Sundays, no matter what the weather. A few slaves received wages, but most received only food and shelter.

Many white people believed God had meant them to hold black people as slaves and that the slaves were happy with their lives in bondage. This was far from true.

Slaves lived in shacks that usually had dirt floors and no fireplaces. Sometimes a dozen people were crowded together under one roof. Slaves were often poorly clothed and fed and were rarely allowed to see a doctor. They were not allowed to marry or to learn to read and write. They were often whipped.

Slaves were bought and sold at public auctions (sales). Slave families were sometimes separated by these auctions.

Slaves were sold and traded, sometimes at public auctions, just as a farmer might sell a cow or a mule. A black boy might be worth $500. A black man and woman together might sell for $1,400. Sometimes a master would split apart a slave family by selling its members to different buyers.

Free Blacks

There were free black people living in Missouri during this time. But their lives were not much better than those of the slaves. Free blacks worked long and hard for little pay and lived in terrible conditions. It was against the law in Missouri for anyone to teach a black person—slave or free—to read or write. This did not always stop people from teaching or learning.

John Berry Meachum was a slave who had managed to save enough money to buy his freedom. A minister, Meachum taught reading and writing during his Sunday school classes until the local sheriff threatened to arrest him if he did not stop. Meachum then bought a steamboat and anchored it in the middle of the Mississippi River. There the sheriff had no power to stop him from teaching blacks to read and write.

The Antislavery Movement

Slavery was important to the state's agricultural economy. But the growing numbers of immigrants from Europe, especially Germany, brought with them a belief that slavery was wrong and should be abolished. They were joined by others who openly worked to end slavery. These people were called **abolitionists**.

The abolitionists disagreed with many of the settlers already in Missouri, especially those who came from slave states such as Virginia, South Carolina, and Tennessee. Most Missourians did not own slaves. But they supported the rights of others to own slaves and the right of the states to decide for themselves whether to allow slavery.

These differences led to conflict between Missouri and Kansas. In 1854, Congress passed a law that **repealed**, or canceled,

Above: John Brown was one of the abolitionist leaders in Kansas. Opposite page: When Abraham Lincoln was elected president in 1860, the southern states began to secede from the Union.

the Missouri Compromise. This new law allowed states formed from the Nebraska and Kansas territories to decide for themselves whether they would be slave states or free states. People argued over whether Kansas would become a slave or a free state.

In 1855, Kansas held an election to choose a territorial legislature. Missourians who favored slavery crossed the border and voted for candidates who were for slavery. Even though there were only 3,000 voters in Kansas, 6,300 ballots were cast in the election! When a Missouri newspaper complained, a proslavery mob threw the newspaper's press into the Missouri River.

Fighting broke out between the abolitionist and proslavery sides in Kansas. Missourians crossed the border to help the proslavery side. Farms and towns were raided and burned to try to scare away abolitionist settlers. State militias and federal troops had to be called in to stop the fighting. Kansas eventually entered the Union as a free state.

Secession

In 1860, Abraham Lincoln was nominated for president of the United States by the Republican party. The Republicans were against slavery. Lincoln campaigned against allowing any new slave states in the Union. The southern states threatened to **secede**, or leave the Union, if Lincoln was elected.

Lincoln did win the election in the fall of 1860. Soon

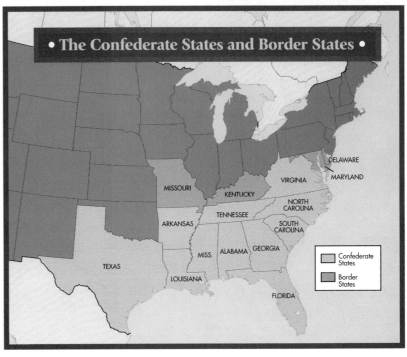

• The Confederate States and Border States •

after, 11 southern states seceded and formed the **Confederate States of America**. On April 12, 1861, Confederate soldiers in South Carolina captured Fort Sumter from Union troops. This event started the Civil War.

Few Missourians wanted Missouri to secede from the United States. But Governor Claiborne Jackson and most of the state government supported the Confederacy. Governor Jackson called out the state militia to fight for the South.

Federal troops from St. Louis rushed to Jefferson City and captured it. Governor Jackson and the legislature fled to Neosho, in southern Missouri. There, on October 28, they voted to join the Confederacy. But federal troops controlled key parts of Missouri, and a government loyal to the Union was set up. Missouri then became a **border state**, a slave state that stayed in the Union. The border states all lay between the North and the South.

Fighting in Missouri

The Civil War divided the state, divided towns, and even divided families. Brothers sometimes found themselves shooting at each other from opposite sides during a battle.

One of every ten battles fought in the Civil War took place in Missouri. The biggest battle was also one of the first, taking place in August 1861. In a very bloody battle along Wilson's

This picture shows the death of Union General Nathaniel Lyon at the Battle of Wilson's Creek in August 1861.

Kansas City

Lexington
Sept. 13-20, 1861

Centralia Massacre
Sept. 27, 1864

Westport
Oct. 23, 1864

St. Louis

Jefferson City

Pilot Knob
Sept. 27, 1864

Wilson's Creek
Aug. 10, 1861

Neosho

• The Civil War in Missouri •

The battle at Lexington in September 1861 has been called the "battle of the hemp bales." Confederate troops soaked the hemp bales in the river. They used the bales as cover and crawled toward the Union line.

Creek near Springfield, the Missouri Confederates defeated the Union Army and chased it back north. One month later, the Confederates again defeated Union forces, this time at Lexington.

The Union Army was able to recover and pushed the Confederates out of Missouri later that winter. The Missouri Confederates then became part of the Confederate Army. For the next three years, the war was fought in Missouri largely between small groups of Union soldiers and small bands of rebels called **bushwhackers**. The bushwhackers raided small towns and farms for supplies—stealing what they could carry and burning the rest—trying to scare the people either into leaving or supporting the South.

Permelia Hardeman wrote down her memories of a bushwhacker raid on her farm in southwest Missouri in 1862.

We were visited last night about two o'clock by the bushwhackers. I was up with the baby when they came. . . . They got both of the guns and then went upstairs, took my bed blankets . . . then searched the bureau drawers. They even took as small a thing as a comb and brush.

Life in the Army

Life was even harder for the soldiers, who had to walk everywhere they went. Often, the wagons carrying their food were delayed or lost. The soldiers were then left with nothing to eat. Sometimes they would steal a cow or pig from a farmer. Many times they had nothing to eat but hardtack. Hardtack was a very hard cracker that had to be soaked in water or coffee to make it soft enough to eat. Often, the hardtack was filled with bugs.

Corporal Philander Nesbit, a Union cavalry soldier fighting in Missouri, wrote home in 1861 to tell his sister about the hard conditions.

These Union soldiers are preparing their dinner. Food was not always easy to come by—for both Union and Confederate troops.

Last week we were out three days without anything to eat, only such as we could pick up. . . . We rode all day and about an hour by sun, stopped at a house and got a piece of corn bread and raw meat which of course tasted like it had been sweetened. We started and rode until ten o'clock and slept in a stable, got up and fed our horses and got no breakfast, rode hard until about ten o'clock and caught up with some infantry. They freely emptied their haversack and gave it to us which consisted of hard crackers.

Confederate soldiers usually had a rough life because the South was short of supplies. A lot of the "Johnny Rebs," as Union soldiers called them, went barefoot, even in winter. There were few doctors in the armies. In those days, there was very little a doctor could do for a person if he or she became sick or was wounded. Many of the people who died in the Civil War died from illness, not from wounds. Corporal Nesbit became sick a few weeks after writing his sister and died four months later.

"Bloody Bill" Anderson was a Confederate bushwacker. He was killed in the Battle of Westport.

Last Chance

The Confederate Army made one last attempt to capture Missouri. In 1864, General Sterling Price invaded from Arkansas. At the same time, small groups of Confederates began attacking towns around the state. One of these groups was led by "Bloody Bill" Anderson. Frank and Jesse James were part of Anderson's gang. They attacked the town of Centralia on September 27, 1864, killing 24 unarmed Union soldiers who were on a train headed home to Iowa. Union troops chased the gang out of town. Then they were ambushed by the Confederates, and 124 more Union soldiers died.

On that same day, General Price's army was attacking Fort Davidson at Pilot Knob. In the Battle of Pilot Knob, wave after wave of Confederate troops rushed toward the fort. They were killed or driven back before they could reach the rock and dirt walls.

Because he lost too many men, General Price changed his mind about attacking St. Louis or Jefferson City. Instead, he marched toward Westport, near Kansas City. On October 23, the Confederate and Union armies finally met in battle. The Confederate forces were defeated. Among the dead was Bloody

Fort Davidson is now a state historic site. The fort was destroyed after the battle. Only the earthworks and these cannon remain.

Bill Anderson. The Battle of Westport marked the end of major fighting in Missouri.

The North had more men, more guns, more factories, and more money than the South. The Confederate Army often won, but it could not replace all the men who died or were wounded nor the supplies it lost. In April 1865, the South surrendered.

In all, there were more than 1,100 battles or **skirmishes** (small clashes) fought in Missouri. Only in Virginia and Tennessee was there more fighting. More than 20,000 Missourians died: 14,000 for the North and at least 6,000 for the South. Much of the state had been raided by the armies. Towns and farms were looted or destroyed. It would be many years before the wounds caused by the war would heal in Missouri.

Sterling Price was governor of Missouri from 1853 to 1857. When fighting broke out in the state, Price joined the Confederate forces and was named a major-general.

Summary

In 1821, Missouri became the 24th state in the Union. As a new state, Missouri had to form a government. It also had to build a strong economy. People had different ways of making a living, but most Missourians lived on farms. It wasn't easy to get around Missouri because of poor roads. Travel improved with the coming of steamboats, stagecoaches, and railroads.

Slavery was a problem—both in Missouri and in the nation. Many people believed slavery was wrong and wanted to abolish it. But others believed they needed slaves to work their farms. Many people believed the question of slavery should be decided by the states and not the federal government.

This disagreement and others split the states, and the North and the South fought the Civil War. Missouri was on the border between North and South, with both sides claiming it. Missourians fought for both sides. Even though the North won the war, the divisions among Missourians remained for a long time.

Chapter • Review

Reviewing Vocabulary

abolitionists
compromise
Confederate States of America
constitution
economy
frontier
secede

On a sheet of paper, write the numbers 1 to 6. Beside each number, write the word or phrase from the list above that best completes the sentence.

1. One way to settle disputes is by a _____, where both sides give a little in their demands.
2. In the 1860s, the southern states voted to _____ from the Union and formed the _____.
3. The _____ involves the jobs people do, what they produce and sell, what they buy, and how they pay for it.
4. People who believed slavery was wrong and wanted to do away with it were called _____.
5. Before Missouri could become a state, it had to write a _____, a list of the rules under which it would operate.
6. The _____ was the area just on the edge of a settled area.

Reviewing Facts

1. What agreement did Congress develop to allow Missouri to become a state?
2. When Missouri became a state, what was its most important industry?
3. Name three types of transportation that people used to travel across Missouri.
4. What two trails started in Missouri?
5. What faster method of moving people and the mail started in Tipton?
6. What event led the southern states to secede from the Union?
7. Was Missouri a southern state or a northern state?
8. Where was the first major Civil War battle in Missouri fought? Where was the last major battle in Missouri fought?

Using What You've Learned

1. Pretend you live on a farm in Missouri in 1820. Draw a picture that tells how you live.
2. Pretend that you are a state legislator working in the first state Capitol in St. Charles. You want to visit the site of the new capital in Jefferson City. How would you get there?

Building Skills

1. Why do you think people wanted to move out onto the frontier?
2. Why do you think some Missourians chose to fight for the Confederacy while others fought for the Union?

Did You Know?

• After the Civil War, Sterling Price chose to leave the United States for Mexico.

Chapter Five

Missouri After the Civil War

The Civil War deeply divided Missourians. Neighbors found themselves fighting against neighbors, friends against friends, and brothers against brothers. The war damaged the state's economy and interrupted the state's growth and progress. The war was over, but could Missourians put their feelings behind them? The slaves had been freed, but what would that freedom bring?

Building Again

The time after the Civil War is called **Reconstruction**. The word *reconstruction* means "building again." Missourians did indeed have to build again, not only their homes and farms, but their towns, their roads, and their government.

Even before the war ended, a new state government had been elected. It was led by a political party called the **Radicals**. One meaning of the word *radical* is a person who acts harshly. The Radicals were people who opposed slavery and who thought those who had supported slavery should in some way be punished.

The first thing the Radicals did was write a new state constitution and laws abolishing slavery. The 1865 constitution had many new ideas that encouraged economic growth and gave people more say in how their state was run.

The 1799 Bollinger Grist Mill at Burfordville was burned during the Civil War. It was rebuilt in brick on the original base. One of Missouri's four covered bridges is at the right.

Top: During the Civil War, Jesse James was a Confederate bushwacker. After the war, he began robbing banks. **Above:** *Jesse James lived in this house in St. Joseph until 1882.*

But while the new constitution outlawed slavery, it did not give blacks—the former slaves—equal rights. They still could not vote or hold government office. The new document also punished former Confederates and people who had supported the Confederacy. It stopped them from voting or holding office. They could not become lawyers or teachers or even ministers. The constitution also required the rest of Missourians to take a **test oath**, swearing that they had never supported the Confederacy.

The U.S. Supreme Court (the highest court in the land) later ruled that the test oath was too harsh a requirement for someone who wanted to be a minister, teacher, or lawyer. But the Court allowed the test oath to remain a requirement to vote or to hold office. The test oath and other punishments in the constitution led to hard feelings. Some former Confederates even felt unwelcome in their home state.

This feeling and the hard economic times caused by the war led some of the former Confederates to become outlaws. Among them were Jesse and Frank James, who robbed banks and held up trains. In some parts of the state, people took the law into their own hands, arresting and punishing people without giving them trials. More than once the only thing a punished person had done was vote for the "wrong" person.

Life After Slavery

For those who had been slaves, the Civil War brought freedom. But it also left them with no homes, no land, and no jobs. The former slaves were largely unwelcome in Missouri. They were driven from some areas by threats of death or serious harm.

Many blacks found themselves working for white farmers as **tenant farmers** in ways that were not much different from slavery. The white landowner gave the tenant farmer a place to live, seed for crops, and the tools to work the land. Sometimes the landowner paid the tenant farmer a wage. The tenant farmer might receive a part of the money earned from selling the crops.

The lives of tenant farmers were only a little better than those of slaves. The houses were usually shacks. There was so little money that the tenant farmer's family often dressed in rags and went hungry. The children rarely went to school because they were needed to work in the fields.

There also were few jobs for black people in the towns, except as servants or laborers. During this time, many black people left Missouri. Some moved to larger cities in the East, where there were more jobs. Some moved to unsettled lands in Kansas and other western states.

Blacks and whites remained **segregated**, or separated by race. They sat in separate sections of churches or went to separate churches altogether. They lived in separate parts of town. Their children went to separate schools.

After the Civil War, many former slaves became tenant farmers. This illustration shows the cabin of a black tenant farming family.

Education

Before the war, education for blacks had been against the law. After the war, schools for blacks were started in many communities. The state provided funding (money) for schools, either white or black, and for the University of Missouri (founded in 1839) for the first time in 1866.

State funding for education was one of the new ideas the Radicals had included in the 1865 constitution. To train teachers for white schools, the state opened teachers' colleges in Kirksville (now Truman State University) and Warrensburg (now Central Missouri State University). Later, another teachers' college was started in Cape Girardeau (now Southeast Missouri State University). Black teachers were trained at Lincoln Institute, a college started in 1866 in Jefferson City by black Civil War veterans. It later became a state school and is now called Lincoln University.

A number of private schools also started in Missouri after the Civil War. Many parts of Missouri did not have high schools after the war. Boys often went to work when they finished the eighth grade. Girls were not expected to work outside the home. A town or a church might start a school called an **academy** for girls to teach them housekeeping, cooking, nursing, and sewing.

Left: Southeast Missouri State in Cape Girardeau started as a teachers' college. *Above:* After the war, the state provided money for the University of Missouri.

Steamboat races were very popular. Perhaps the most famous was the 1870 race from New Orleans to St. Louis between the Natchez *and the* Robert E. Lee. *The* Robert E. Lee *won.*

Sometimes the academy also had religious classes. Often, the academy became a junior college when a high school was finally built in the town.

Cultural Activities

Better public education encouraged more and more people to improve other parts of their lives. Many communities started libraries. Other communities built lecture halls and concert halls. People in the towns could go there to hear speeches and music, to see plays, and even to watch circus acts.

Missourians had fun at various sports, such as ice skating, bike riding, hunting, fishing, horse racing, and a new sport—baseball. There were also steamboat races on the Mississippi River.

The first county fair west of the Mississippi had been held in Boone County in 1835. After the Civil War, county fairs became very popular. Farmers would show off their best animals and crops. Merchants from town would show off their goods.

Top: *Bicycles in the late 1800s looked very different from those of today. This photograph was taken in 1889.* **Left:** *Mount Vernon Church was built in 1871 in Excelsior Springs. People who worked at the Watkins Woolen Mill worshiped here.*

Religion became even more important to Missourians after the Civil War. Church membership grew as more ministers settled in the state. The number of churches in Missouri doubled in the first **decade** (a period of 10 years) after the war to more than 3,000.

Missouri's beauty and life on the frontier inspired a number of artists and writers living in Missouri. One famous painter was George Caleb Bingham. He painted scenes of life along the Missouri River near his home in Arrow Rock and portraits of famous people. Perhaps the most famous writer of the pe-

Right: George Caleb Bingham painted this portrait of himself in 1835. *Left:* Bingham lived in this house in Arrow Rock from 1837 to 1845.

Left: This photograph of Samuel Clemens ("Mark Twain") was taken in 1874. He had already published Roughing It, *a part of which appeared on page 82. Below: Eugene Field was born in St. Louis. He worked as a newspaper reporter and columnist. But he is best known for his children's poetry.*

riod was Samuel Clemens, who was better known as Mark Twain. Clemens was born in the small Missouri town of Florida, but he grew up in Hannibal. Many of his stories, such as *Tom Sawyer* and *The Adventures of Huckleberry Finn*, were about growing up and working on the Mississippi River.

A famous Missouri poet after the Civil War was Eugene Field, a newspaper reporter who wrote poetry for children. Among his poems were "Little Boy Blue" and "Wynken, Blynken, and Nod."

Rebuilding the Economy

The 35 years after the Civil War saw tremendous changes in Missouri. In that period, the state went from a frontier wilderness to one of the country's major manufacturing states. **Manufacturing** involves taking a natural resource, such as wood, and turning it into a product, such as furniture.

Railroads

Railroads were just beginning to cross Missouri when the Civil War stopped much of the work. After the war, railroad construction boomed (grew rapidly). St. Louis became an important rail center. Rail lines were completed between St. Louis and Kansas City, St. Louis and Springfield, and St. Louis and Arkansas.

Rivers had been important transportation routes in the days of keelboats and steamboats. But they were obstacles (something in the way) for the railroads. Bridges had to be built over the Missouri and Mississippi rivers. Important railroad bridges were built in Kansas City and at Hannibal and St. Charles. Famous bridges were built at Glasgow and St. Louis. The Glasgow bridge over the Missouri River was the first all-steel bridge. The Eads Bridge in St. Louis was the first to use steel arches. The Eads Bridge was also the first built over the Mississippi River at St. Louis. Workers had to brave a dangerous river

Left: The Eads Bridge over the Mississippi River opened in 1874. It is the oldest bridge still crossing the river. Today it carries light rail trains. **Above:** St. Louis in the 1880s was a busy rail center and river port.

current and dig 90 feet down to solid rock to anchor the supports for the bridge. Several workers died during construction.

New towns, such as Sedalia and Joplin, grew up along the railroads, especially where two lines crossed or a rail line branched out. The railroads turned a number of small towns into big cities. Springfield, for example, went from just over 3,000 residents in 1860 to nearly 22,000 in 1890. Larger cities grew even faster. St. Louis doubled in size between 1860 and 1870. By the turn of the century, it had more than a half

In 1860, Eberhard Anheuser and his son-in-law, Adolphus Busch, took over a small local business and turned it into the world's largest brewer.

million people and was the eighth-largest city in the country.

Manufacturing and Mining

The railroads made it possible to ship raw materials to factories and mills. **Raw materials** are any materials that are processed to make another product. The railroads then shipped the manufactured goods from the factories and mills to buyers all over the country.

Kansas City became famous for its large **stockyards**, where cattle, pigs, horses, and mules were bought and sold. Meat-packing plants were built alongside the stockyards and meat was shipped around the country in refrigerated rail cars. Kansas City was also an important grain center. Wheat, corn, and oats were shipped in and turned into flour, cornmeal, corn syrup, and oatmeal.

St. Louis was important for its iron mills, breweries, and clothing, furniture, and shoe factories. St. Louis also was home to leading manufacturers of street cars, chemicals, medicine, and bricks.

Smaller cities also had factories. Hannibal was famous for cigars and boats; Springfield for cotton, woolen goods, and wagons; and St. Joseph for meat packing.

Mining grew in importance in Missouri during this time. There were large lead mines around Bonne Terre and Joplin, and limestone quarries around St. Louis and Carthage. There were coal mines in northeast and west-central Missouri. Clay for bricks was found near Fulton and Mexico. Mining was so important that the state legislature created a School of Mines in Rolla.

Agriculture

With railroads reaching most parts of Missouri, farmers could now farm more land because it was easier to ship crops and livestock to market. The number of farms in Missouri grew, from 93,000 in 1860 to 238,000 in 1890. The average-sized farm was about 130 acres.

Farming was also easier because of new machinery, such as threshers, and better plows and planters. Horses and mules still supplied most of the power, but steam-driven tractors were beginning to take over some of the work. By 1890, Missouri farmers grew 5 times more corn, 10 times more oats, and 9 times more wheat than they had in 1866.

Other important crops were cotton in the Bootheel, tobacco and hemp along the Missouri River, and grapes and fruit trees in the Ozarks and along the Missouri River.

Farmers received help from experts at the College of Agriculture in Columbia and at the State Board of Agriculture. They traded ideas and shared their knowledge at county fairs and in the many magazines and weekly newspapers written for farmers and their families.

Lumbering and sawmills were important in southern Missouri. **Lumberjacks** (those whose job it is to cut and prepare timber) built railroads into the pine forests, set up a sawmill, and cut down all the trees they could find. Then they tore up the railroad tracks, tore down the sawmill, and moved to the next forest. After a while, most of the pine trees were gone, and the lumber companies moved on to other states.

In the late 1800s, new equipment such as the steam tractor made life easier for Missouri farmers. This steam tractor is on display in Ste. Genevieve.

Zithers and Corn Cob Pipes

Many of the goods manufactured in Missouri were also made in other states. But there were two items made in Missouri and probably nowhere else: the zither and the corn cob pipe. Both were made in Washington, a town along the Missouri River.

A *zither* is a stringed instrument that looks like a long, narrow guitar. It has 30 to 40 strings attached to a hollow box. A person plays a zither by placing it in his or her lap or on a table and plucking the strings with the fingers or a guitar pick.

The first American-made zithers were made in Washington in 1866 by Franz Schwarzer. His zithers were world famous. Schwarzer won a gold medal at an 1873 fair in Vienna, Austria. The Washington zithers were made of woods from around the world. They could be very fancy and expensive or very plain and affordable for most families. Zither players would gather in the city park in Washington on Sunday afternoons and play concerts.

FRANZ SCHWARZER

Maker of Fine Zithers and Mandolins.
The most extensive plant devoted to the manufacture of Zithers in America.
WASHINGTON, MO.

Top: Franz Schwarzer began making zithers in Washington in 1866. Above: This ad shows you what a zither looks like. Opposite page: Henry Tibbe (top) produced corn cob pipes at this factory in Washington (below).

The zither was not as popular in the 1900s, and few were made after the 1920s. The factory where they were made was finally torn down in 1950.

When German immigrants settled along the Missouri River near Washington, they couldn't find any *meerschaum*. That is a white clay found in Europe that is used to make pipes for smoking. In 1869, pipe maker Henry Tibbe thought of using corn cobs. He cut the cobs into short pieces. Then he hollowed out the center to have a place for the tobacco. Finally, he drilled a hole for the stem. To make the pipes look like those in Germany, Tibbe covered them with Missouri clay and polished them smooth. Some people laughed and called corn cobs "Missouri meerschaum," so that's what Tibbe called his company. The pipes were very popular and were soon being shipped to other parts of the country and overseas.

Many famous people have smoked Missouri Meerschaum pipes, including General Douglas MacArthur. Today, they are popular as souvenirs. The Missouri Meerschaum Company still makes 18 styles of corn cob pipes. Washington is known as the "Corn Cob Pipe Capital of the World."

Telephones and Electricity

We take for granted that we will have lights in the dark and that we can call our friends on the telephone whenever we please. But just 125 years ago, electric lights and telephones were still rare and enjoyed by only a few.

In the years after the Civil War, most families still relied on candles and lanterns for light. Farm families often went to bed shortly after sundown and awoke before dawn. In that way, they were able to start work as soon as the sun was up and it was light outside.

In the cities, candles and lanterns were still used. But many houses, businesses, and factories had gas lights. The gas was found underground in wells or produced by heating coal. It was piped into homes and other buildings. Gas also was used to light street lamps. Men called lamplighters went around at dusk to light the lamps and then turned them off at dawn.

Electricity was only beginning to be used. Before 1890, few houses or buildings were wired for electricity or connected to an electrical line. Electric lights and other appliances were rare.

Telephones were more common. The first long-distance call made from Missouri was placed in Cape Girardeau in 1877. Hannibal became the first city in Missouri to have a telephone exchange, a network of wires connecting homes and businesses. By 1885, telephone lines linked Kansas City to St. Louis. By 1890, most large cities and many small towns in Missouri were linked by telephone.

Life in the City

For young boys or girls on the farm, life in the city seemed glamorous and exciting compared to their lives of getting up early, doing chores, going to school, and going to bed early. But life in the city was often hard and dangerous.

The cities were crowded as more and more people moved from the farms or came to America as immigrants from other

In the 1890s, Kansas City was a busy, bustling city. This view is of Main Street.

In the late 1800s, tenement buildings were not usually rundown, but they were close together. This view is of the back of some tenements in St. Louis. Notice that there are no fire escapes.

countries. Only the wealthier people had houses. Most families lived in buildings called **tenements**. Tenements are like apartment buildings, but they usually only had three or four families in each building.

The buildings were three or four stories high, sometimes higher, with one family living on top of another. Each family had perhaps a kitchen, a family room, and a couple of bedrooms. All of the families might share one bathroom in the building, although many of the buildings did not have indoor plumbing.

The buildings were very close to one another and right next to the street. The children played on the sidewalks or in the streets. The streets could be dangerous because they were filled with horse-drawn wagons and coaches.

Most children went to school. When they were old enough to work, many quit and joined their fathers, brothers, and sometimes mothers and sisters in the factories. They often did dangerous jobs and were injured or killed by the machinery. The children worked as many as 12 hours a day, sometimes for as little as 25 cents a day. In the winter, the factories were damp and cold. In the summer, they were hot and sweaty. They were always noisy. The air was filled with lint, dust, or smoke.

Because so many factories burned coal for power or heat, the air in the cities was dirty and unhealthy. Because people lived and worked so close together, when someone became ill the illness soon spread in an **epidemic** to many other people in the community. There were none of the modern medicines we have today. Many people, including many children, died from diseases that are easily cured or prevented today.

But there were fun times too. Families rode the horse-drawn streetcars or walked to the city parks on Sundays. Some took buggy rides into the country to see the farms and have picnics. There were sports to watch, games to play, and theaters and libraries to visit.

Life could also be colorful, with so many immigrants speaking different languages. Markets were filled with many kinds of fruits and vegetables. Department stores were filled with all kinds

A community picnic was a popular way to celebrate the Fourth of July in the 1890s. This picnic took place in Williamsburg.

Not all city dwellers lived in tenements in the late 1800s. This is Vaile House in Independence. It was the 30-room house of a local businessman.

of goods. People selling peanuts or collecting old rags went up and down the street yelling or singing to attract customers.

Summary

After the Civil War, the people of Missouri had to rebuild—their homes, their businesses, their towns and cities, and their government. There were many hard feelings. Some of the laws passed by the new government were written to punish people who had supported the Confederate states.

Most Missourians still lived and worked on farms. Railroads helped the farmers ship their crops and livestock to market. The railroads also helped factories grow in the cities. The cities became bigger and attracted people from the farms and from other countries.

The end of the Civil War brought an end to slavery in Missouri. While they had their freedom, many black Missourians did not see their lives become better because there were few or only low-paying jobs for them. Many became tenant farmers.

New inventions like the telephone helped Missouri grow and made it an important manufacturing state. The state was very different in 1890 than it had been at the end of the Civil War.

Chapter • Review

Reviewing Vocabulary

academies
epidemic
lumberjack
raw materials
segregated
tenant farmer
tenements

On a sheet of paper, write the numbers 1 to 7. Beside each number, write the word or phrase from the list above that best completes the sentence.

1. A person who cuts down trees for a sawmill is called a _____.
2. Many people who lived in the cities lived in _____.
3. A _____ works on a farm in exchange for a place to live and a share of the crops.
4. _____ are sent to factories, where they are turned into manufactured goods.
5. When disease quickly spreads among many people, we call it an _____.
6. _____ were started to educate girls after the Civil War.
7. Even though the slaves had been freed, blacks and whites were _____ in Missouri.

Reviewing Facts

1. Why is the period after the Civil War called "Reconstruction"?
2. Why were those elected to the state government after the Civil War called "Radicals"?
3. What teachers' college was started by black Civil War veterans?
4. What happened to the cattle and pigs sold at the Kansas City stockyards?
5. Name at least four products manufactured in Missouri in the period after the Civil War.
6. Name three things mined in Missouri.
7. How did people light their homes before electricity?
8. Why was factory work sometimes dangerous for children?

Using What You've Learned

1. Look at a map of Missouri that shows both towns and railroad lines. Which towns do you think were probably started because of the railroads?
2. Look around your bedroom and make a list of all the things you have. How many of these things do you think a student your age would have had in 1890?

Building Skills

1. If you were growing up in 1880, would you rather have lived on a farm or in the city? Why?
2. Why were blacks denied the right to vote after Reconstruction?

Did You Know?

- The first all-steel bridge in the world was built over the Missouri River at Glasgow in 1878.

This picture of an early automobile was taken in 1903 on a road just outside Joplin. Traffic on the roads in those days was very light.

Chapter Six

A Changing Missouri

Aperson born the year Missouri applied for statehood—1820—would have traveled his or her whole life by horse and probably would have died 70 years later without ever having seen an automobile. But a person born that same year—1890—would have grown up seeing not only automobiles, but also airplanes, spaceships to the moon, television, and computers. How have Missourians kept up with so many changes?

The Beginnings of an Urban Society

Cities and their surrounding towns, you will remember, are called urban areas. The areas outside the cities are called rural areas. For most of its history, Missouri was considered a rural state because most of its people lived or worked on farms or in very small towns and villages.

Automobiles Come to Missouri

Try to imagine your family not having an automobile. You would probably stay home more and maybe never leave your town except for special trips. Well, before 1890, there were no automobiles in Missouri. Most people traveled by horse, horse-drawn wagon, or streetcar. Long trips often meant a ride on a train or a riverboat.

Because travel was so hard and slow, most people did not go far from home. The automobile changed all that, although in the early days, travel by "horseless carriage" was not very easy either. One reason is that the roads outside of the cities were

Road service did not exist in the early 1900s. When this car got stuck in a creek, the young man had to get out and push.

still mostly dirt or gravel. They turned to mud whenever it rained or snowed. An automobile driver could spend most of a trip pushing the car out of the mud. Sometimes the driver needed the help of a farmer and a mule!

As more and more people bought cars, they complained more and more about the bad roads. In 1920, a campaign called "Lift Missouri Out of the Mud" was started. The state took over the building and repairing of most roads. New taxes were passed to pay for the new paved roads and bridges. **Taxes** are the money paid by people and businesses to the government to pay for the services the government provides.

The automobile and better roads brought a lot of changes to Missouri. Places to eat, places to stay for the night, tourist attractions, and gasoline stations were among the new businesses. Going to town was faster and easier. It also was easier for the doctor to make house calls and for the mail carrier to deliver the mail.

Not all of the changes were good. People didn't stay home or do things together as a family as much. Instead of going to the small general store in their village, people could now go to the big department stores in the cities. Many general stores closed. Some of the small towns around them disappeared. Faster cars meant more accidents. To enforce safe driving laws, the State Highway Patrol was started in 1931.

Changes on the Farm

At the same time Missourians were dealing with the changes brought by automobiles, new machinery was bringing changes to the farm. Gasoline-powered tractors began replacing steam-driven tractors and mules and horses. These tractors meant a farmer could do more work with fewer workers.

Despite the new machinery and other improvements in farming, times were not good for farmers in the early 1900s.

In the early 1900s, gasoline-powered tractors replaced the steam-powered tractor. Compare this photograph with the photograph on page 113.

The Louisiana Purchase Centennial Exposition

We get excited when we hear about a new type of computer or a new and faster airplane or a robot that can make a CD player. If someone told us there was going to be a fair where we could see all of these new and wonderful things and much more, we would probably make plans to attend.

Well, that's what happened in 1904 at the Louisiana Purchase Centennial Exposition or, simply, the St. Louis World's Fair. More than 19 million people came to the fair from all over the country and around the world. It was supposed to celebrate 100 years of history since the Louisiana Purchase. But it was really a peek at the future.

There were hundreds of buildings built just for the fair. In the buildings, people could see the newest inventions, demonstrations of electricity, and the latest automobiles. One building had 14 miles of railroad tracks in it! Other buildings were filled with displays of art and flowers. There were restaurants

*Above: In this photograph of the Louisiana Purchase Centennial Exposition you can see the Grand Basin and St. Louis Plaza. **Left:** These Sioux Indians appeared and performed at the Fair. **Opposite page below:** The only building that still remains from the Fair is now home to the St. Louis Art Museum.*

and concert halls. Different nations built buildings to show off items from their countries. Whole villages of Indian and African tribes were built on the fairgrounds, and people could see how the villagers lived.

There was plenty of fun too. Fair-goers could row boats in a lake built just for the fair or walk through a cage of tropical birds. They could ride on a Ferris wheel that had 36 cars; each car carried 60 passengers more than 250 feet into the air.

Fair-goers could also sample new foods, such as ice cream cones, hot dogs, and iced tea. The fair lasted seven months. When it was over, most of the buildings were torn down. The Ferris wheel was blown up. Most of the land became a park, and the bird cage became part of the zoo.

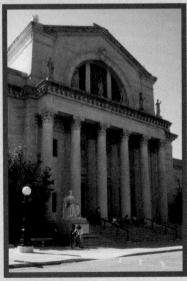

The prices farmers received for their crops and livestock continued to go down. The costs for the new machinery kept going up. Many farmers went deeper and deeper into debt. Others gave up and moved to the cities.

The need for fewer workers, farmers who gave up and left the farm, farm children who decided that farming had no future—all of these shifted Missouri's population to urban areas. In 1920, 53 percent of Missourians lived in rural communities. By 1930, only 49 percent did.

Political Changes

The farmers' troubles led many of them to band together in **cooperatives**, or groups that shared profits and costs. One such cooperative was the Missouri Farmers Association, which started in 1917. The cooperatives built grain elevators to store the harvests and sold seed and other supplies to farmers at prices they could afford.

Other farmers looked to government for help and change. Some joined with others to form a new political party. Members of this new party were called **Populists** because they considered their ideas to be those of the common people. The Populists won few elections, but other politicians listened to their ideas and many of those ideas became laws. One law kept railroads from charging farmers too much to haul grain to market. Another made it illegal for companies to allow children under age 14 to work in dangerous factory and mine jobs.

The Populists were followed by the **Progressives**, who believed that government should help make life better for everyone. The Progressives were more successful than the Populists at winning elections and making changes. They passed laws to help the poor, to protect children, to make sure that food sold in stores was safe, and to force businesses to treat people fairly. The Progressives believed education was important. They worked to pass a law that required all children between the ages of 8 and 14 to go to school. They also started teachers' colleges in Springfield (now Southwest Missouri State University) and Maryville (now Northwest Missouri State University).

Northwest Missouri State University in Maryville was started as a college to train teachers.

World War I and the 1920s

In the early 1900s, Americans were busy working with all of the changes in their lives. Europeans, however, were troubled by problems that eventually led them—and America—into war.

Americans at War

When the fighting in Europe started in August 1914, most Americans wanted to be **neutral**; that is, we wanted to stay out of the fighting. In the war, Germany and its allies fought Great Britain, France, and their allies. The United States became involved when the German navy began sinking merchant ships, some of them carrying Americans. The United States entered the war in April 1917 on the side of Great Britain.

In April 1917, citizens in Boonville turned out to support the United States's declaration of war.

It was a hard time for Missourians whose families had come from Germany. In some towns, German street names were changed to English names. Schools stopped teaching the German language. Many of the German-language newspapers in Missouri went out of business or changed to English. Some people even refused to eat sauerkraut, or they called it "liberty cabbage."

The war ended in November 1918. With the help of the American soldiers, the British and French were able to defeat Germany and its allies. More than 156,000 Missourians fought in the war, including many black soldiers and Captain Harry Truman.

The American troops in Europe were led by General John Pershing, a Missourian. General Pershing was called "Black Jack" by his soldiers because he had once commanded a regiment of black troops. General Pershing was born and grew up in Laclede in northwest Missouri in a house that is now a state historic site.

Missourians helped win the war in many ways. They supplied the army with food, weapons, and other supplies. Missouri also sent more than 6,000 mules to Europe to help carry all those supplies.

Prohibition

Not everyone was busy fighting the war in Europe. Ever since the Civil War, groups of Missourians had fought for **prohibition**, laws that would make the production, sale, and use of alcoholic beverages illegal. These people believed that alcohol was the cause of violence, accidents, and other problems.

In 1919, the states, including Missouri, **ratified** (approved) the Eighteenth Amendment to the U.S. Constitution. An **amendment** is an official addition to a document. Before an amendment can become part of the Constitution, three-fourths of the states must ratify it. The Eighteenth Amendment made the manufacture or sale of alcohol illegal. This law was hard on Missouri because the state had several wineries and dozens of breweries.

The new amendment did not remain popular, however. One reason was that some people continued to make alcohol and sell it. This was illegal and led to other crimes and violence. In 1933, the states ratified the Twenty-first Amendment, which repealed the Eighteenth Amendment. Alcoholic beverages were once again legal.

The Great Depression

Life was exciting in the 1920s. There were more and faster cars. There were airplanes, radios, phonographs, and motion pictures (called *silent movies* because they did not have sound). There were new inventions and new electrical appliances for the home.

Above: General John J. Pershing, on the right, was photographed with Marshall Joseph Joffre, president of France. Opposite page top: Many died in World War I in part because of new weapons such as the machine gun. Opposite page below: Harry Truman was a captain during World War I.

But not everything was well. Farmers continued to struggle because of low crop prices, high costs for farm supplies, and growing **debt** (money owed to others). Factories were producing more and more goods. But people could not afford to buy them. The war in Europe left many of those nations too poor to buy American goods. The American economy was like a house made of cards—it would not take much to knock it down.

The Depression Begins

Companies often sell **stock**, which gives buyers a share of the ownership of the company. When the company does well, the stock price goes up. The buyers can then make a profit if they sell the stock for more than they paid for it.

During the 1920s, the price of stocks kept going up and up, even if the companies were not doing well. Many people were buying stocks on **credit**. That is, they borrowed the money to buy the stock expecting to pay back the borrowed money when they sold the stock at a profit.

In October 1929, the stock market—where shares of stock are bought and sold—"crashed." Stock prices started falling. People rushed to sell their stock before they lost too much money. Stock prices plunged. People owning the stocks lost money and could not pay back the money they had borrowed. Some people lost everything.

*Above: This tenant farmer's daughter is reading on the bed in the living room of her family's cabin. **Opposite page:** The Farm Security Administration was established in 1935 to help farmers, such as this New Madrid tenant farmer, during the Great Depression.*

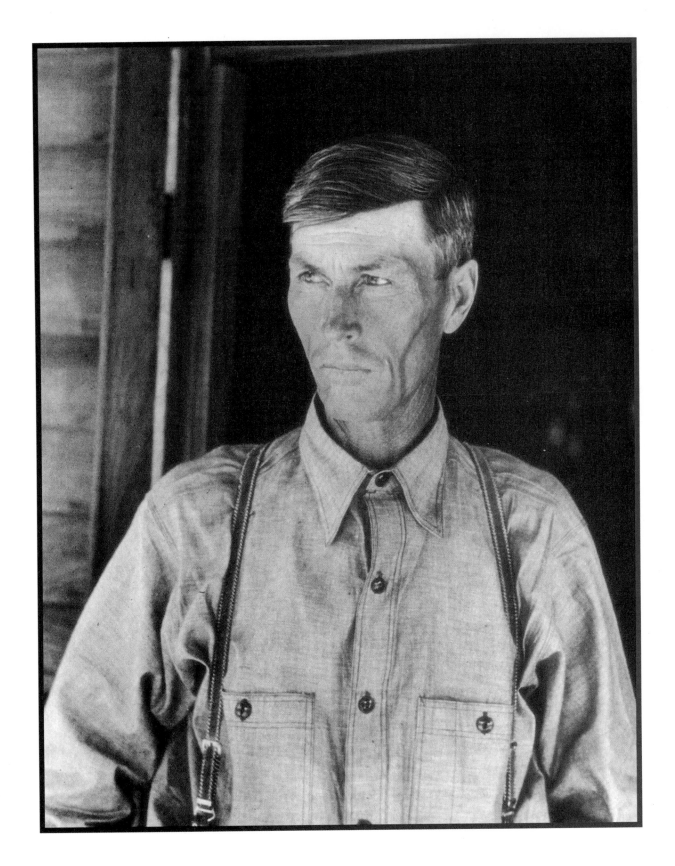

The stock market crash was a sign that there were serious problems in the economy. Businesses began to lay off workers or close. Unemployed workers could no longer buy cars or houses and the furniture and appliances for those houses. That caused more companies to close. The unemployed workers could not buy as much food, so farmers suffered even more. Soon, farmers and the unemployed workers could not pay back the money they had borrowed from banks to buy their tractors and cars and houses.

With too few borrowers paying back their loans, banks went out of business. People who had savings and checking accounts in the banks lost all their money. Without money, they could not buy goods and food. Still more businesses and farmers went broke.

When this happens, we say the economy is in a **depression**, like a balloon that has lost all of its air. There have been other depressions in our country's history, but never were so many people and businesses affected so severely. That is why the period from 1929 to 1941 is called "the Great Depression."

Top: During the Great Depression, many tenant farmers could not pay their rent and were evicted from their farms. This evicted farmer in Butler County is reading his bible. Above: Franklin Roosevelt campaigned for president in 1932 with the promise of a "New Deal" to help end the depression.

The New Deal

More than one-fourth of working Missourians lost their jobs in the Great Depression. Those who still had jobs were only making half of what they used to make. People stood in long lines waiting for handouts of food. Others lost their homes and had to live in tents or shacks. Something had to be done.

In 1932, Franklin Roosevelt was elected president of the United States. He had a number of ideas about how to help people and help the country get out of the Depression. He called his ideas the **New Deal**.

Many New Deal programs put people to work building roads and public buildings. Drive around Missouri today and you will see many county courthouses, schools, parks, swimming pools, and roads built by these workers. Other workers planted trees and worked on other projects to help the environment.

Many farmers lost their farms and became tenant farmers or moved to the cities. But some of the New Deal programs helped farmers too. When the Depression started, most farmers did not have electricity. One New Deal program brought electricity to rural Missouri, making farmers' lives easier.

Life Goes On

Even though times were hard and people were poor, there was still much to do that was fun. One favorite activity was listening to the radio. Missouri's first radio station was WEW in St. Louis. It was only the second station in the country when it went on the air in 1921. The radio had soap operas and cooking shows, music and talk shows, news and speeches, and regular programs.

Families would sit around the radio in the evening and listen to their favorite programs. A favorite comedy program was "Fibber McGee and Molly." Every time Fibber opened his closet, everything fell out. Radio had no pictures, so the listeners had to use their imaginations to "see" all of the junk they could hear falling on Fibber's head. Listeners' imaginations and eerie sound effects could make a scary program like "The Shadow" even scarier or an adventure program like "The Lone Ranger" even more exciting.

Movies were also popular during the Depression. On Saturday afternoons, kids could pay a nickel and see cartoons and a western movie. In many towns, the movie theater was the only building with air-conditioning, which made it very popular in the summer. Movie theaters also doubled as stages, where traveling entertainers would perform skits and music. This type of entertainment was called "vaudeville."

One New Deal program brought electricity to rural areas. This man is stringing electrical lines in Hayti.

Music

Missouri is famous for two types of music that developed after the turn of the century. The first was **ragtime**, a blend of Negro spirituals, march music, and popular tunes played with a quick beat, usually on a piano. One of the most famous ragtime composers was Scott Joplin, who lived in Sedalia for a short time and later in St. Louis. He wrote several well-known ragtime tunes. "The Maple Leaf Rag" was named after a tavern in Sedalia where he played piano. "The Entertainer" was used as the theme song for the movie *The Sting*. Joplin's house in St. Louis is now a state historic site.

The second type of music was the **blues**, a music style based on black folk music. The blues didn't begin in Missouri, but many famous blues singers, performers, and composers were

Above: Scott Joplin lived in this house (top) in St. Louis in 1902. You can listen to his songs in the music room.
Right: T. S. Eliot was born in Missouri in 1888. Later he moved to England and became a British citizen.

from or lived in Missouri. One of them was W. C. Handy, who spent some time in St. Louis and later wrote "The St. Louis Blues."

Other forms of music were popular as well. Many homes had phonographs to play records. Most towns had a band that performed on a bandstand in the middle of the town park each Sunday afternoon or on holidays.

Literature

Reading remained a favorite pastime for many people. One of the most-read books during this time was *Shepherd of the Hills* by Harold Bell Wright. He used his experiences as a city-born minister working in the Ozarks to create his stories.

St. Louis was the birthplace of three famous poets from this time. Sara Teasdale wrote poems about love. Marianne Moore often wrote about nature. T. S. Eliot later moved to England but still wrote about events from his life in Missouri. Some of his poems were the basis for the musical *Cats*.

Baseball

Missourians enjoyed many sports after the turn of the century and through the Depression. The most popular was probably baseball. St. Louis had two major league teams—the Cardinals and the Browns.

The Cardinals won the National League pennant in 1926 and 1928 and won the World Series in 1930, 1931, and 1934. In the 1930s, the team was sometimes called "the Gas House Gang" and was led by Dizzy Dean and his brother Paul, both pitchers. In 1944, the Cardinals won the World Series again, beating the Browns.

Only white players were allowed on major league teams. Black players formed the Negro Leagues. One of the best Negro League teams was the Kansas City Monarchs, led by pitcher Satchel Paige. It was said that Paige was so fast that he could turn off the bedroom light and be back in bed before the room turned dark!

Top: Sara Teasdale, born in St. Louis in 1884, won a Pulitzer Prize for her poetry. **Above:** *In 1934, Dizzy Dean (left) and his brother Paul (right) won 48 games in the regular season. This photograph was taken during the 1934 World Series, which the Cardinals won.*

World War II

The Great Depression happened not just in the United States but all over the world. It was much worse in some countries. In places like Germany, Italy, the Soviet Union, and Japan, people became very discouraged. Their governments could not help. They allowed **dictators** to take over. Those dictators did not allow people to have a say in what their governments did. People who disagreed with them were often killed or sent to prison.

When things did not get better in their countries, the dictators blamed other countries. They convinced their people that the only way to better times was to attack the other countries.

In September 1939, Germany and the Soviet Union attacked Poland. Great Britain and France declared war on Germany and the Soviet Union and their ally, Italy. Soon the nations of Europe were again at war, in what came to be called World War II. Again, the United States tried to stay neutral.

But on December 7, 1941, the naval base at Pearl Harbor, Hawaii, was attacked by Japan, an ally of Germany. The United States declared war on Japan the next day, and Germany declared war on us. Now Americans were at war, not only in Europe, but all across the Pacific Ocean.

Missourians at War Again

Missourians responded by enlisting in the armed forces. Others went to work in factories making the guns, airplanes, tanks, and other materials needed for the war. Factories that used to make shoes for boys and girls started making boots for soldiers. Factories that made cars started making airplane parts. Tractor factories made tanks. Fertilizer plants made explosives.

So many materials were needed to fight the war that the government **rationed**, or limited the use of, many items. It rationed tires and food, gasoline and paper, and a long list of other things. People drove less to conserve tires and fuel.

Communities held scrap drives to collect used materials to **recycle** (reuse) into new materials. Old tires were cut up and

Missouri artist Thomas Hart Benton painted this picture entitled "Embarkation" in 1942. It was part of a series of paintings about World War II entitled Year of Peril.

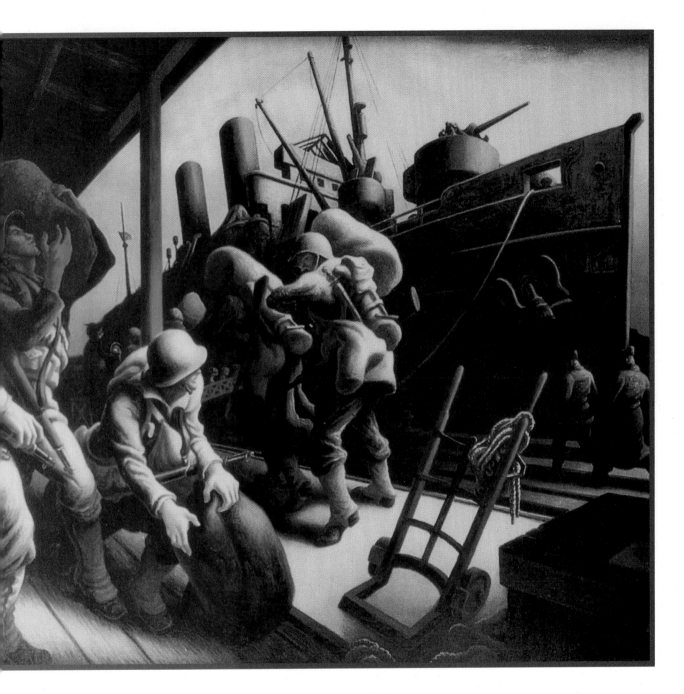

made into new tires. Old pots and pans, cars, and other scrap metal were melted down to make steel for bullets and ships. Cooking grease was saved to make explosives. Schoolchildren collected scrap metal and rags. They also collected pennies, and their parents saved their dollars to buy war bonds. The bonds helped the government pay for the war.

Above: The United States entered World War II when Japan attacked the naval base at Pearl Harbor, Hawaii.

Because so many men were away fighting the war, women began working in factories and on the railroads. They did jobs that only men had done before the war.

Among the many men and women from Missouri fighting in the war was General Omar Bradley. He was born in Clark and went to school in nearby Moberly in north-central Missouri. General Bradley worked closely with General Dwight Eisenhower, the commander of the Allied troops in Europe.

Top right: *German dictator Adolf Hitler after the fall of Paris, France.* **Middle right:** *These American troops are wading ashore on D-Day.* **Bottom right:** *Japanese surrender papers were signed aboard the U.S.S. Missouri.*

Harry S Truman

Missourian Harry S Truman was elected vice president in 1944. In 1945, he became president when Franklin Roosevelt died in office.

Harry Truman was born in Lamar, in southwest Missouri, but grew up in Independence. After fighting in World War I, he started a business selling hats and shirts. He was later elected a county official in Jackson County.

Truman was a hard worker and well liked by people who met him. His hard work and friendliness helped him to be elected a U.S. senator in 1934. He continued to work hard in Washington and led a committee that helped save the government money in buying materials for the war.

In 1944, President Roosevelt picked Truman to be his vice president. It was a surprise choice, because few people outside of Washington or Missouri knew much about him. But in April 1945, President Roosevelt died and Vice President Harry Truman became president.

His first job as president was to finish the war. It was President Truman's decision to use atomic bombs on Japan. It was a hard decision, but Harry Truman never avoided hard decisions. His motto was "The buck stops here," meaning he accepted the responsibility.

The atomic bombs forced Japan to surrender in August 1945. The papers ending the war were signed on the battleship *U.S.S. Missouri* in Tokyo Bay. After the war ended, President Truman led the country as it tried to return to normal.

Many people did not think President Truman would be re-elected in 1948. Some newspapers even printed stories on election night saying that he had lost. But he surprised everyone by winning. His second term in office was a good time for the country, but also a time filled with many more hard decisions and a war in Korea.

When his term ended in 1953, the former president returned to Independence. There he could be seen taking a walk each day and working at his library. If you visit the library, you can learn more about the only Missourian to be elected president.

Many people—and some newspapers—were surprised when President Truman was re-elected in 1948.

Summary

In this chapter, you learned that the first half of the twentieth century was a time of great change in Missouri. New inventions

*Below: Harry Truman lived in this farmhouse in Grandview from 1906 until 1917. **Right:** This house in Independence was home to Harry and Bess Truman from 1919 until their deaths. It is now a national historic site.*

like the automobile and the gasoline-powered tractor brought about many changes, including a shift from a rural population to an urban one.

Missourians played important roles in fighting two world wars as well as in developing new types of music and in writing wonderful poetry. Despite hard times, Missourians did not give up during the Depression. They found ways to work and ways to have fun.

Harry Truman, a Missourian, became president of the United States and led the country during difficult and changing times.

Chapter • Review

Reviewing Vocabulary

cooperatives
credit
neutral
prohibition
ragtime
ratified
taxes

On a sheet of paper, write the numbers 1 to 7. Beside each number, write the word from the list above that best completes each sentence.

1. Struggling farmers formed _____, which built grain elevators and sold farm supplies.
2. If you buy something on _____, you can pay for it later.
3. If you try not to take sides during a fight, you are trying to be _____.
4. In the early 1900s, Missouri passed _____ to raise money to build and repair roads.
5. A popular type of music that developed in Missouri was _____.
6. _____ made it illegal to make, sell, or use alcoholic beverages.
7. Amendments must be _____ by the states before becoming a part of the U.S. Constitution.

Reviewing Facts

1. Why did farmers have a hard time in the early 1900s?
2. What are some of the reasons that led Missourians to move to the cities?
3. Who led the American troops in Europe in World War I?
4. What happens in a depression?
5. How did the New Deal programs help people and the economy?
6. What did people do for fun during the Great Depression?
7. Why did the government have to ration things during World War II?
8. When did Harry Truman become president and why?
9. Why did President Truman say "The buck stops here"?

Using What You've Learned

1. Make a list of the changes that resulted as more and more people bought cars.
2. What were some of the laws the Populists and Progressives passed and how did those laws help people?

Building Skills

1. Why did some countries allow dictators to take over during the early 1900s? Why did that not happen in the United States?
2. Why was President Truman's decision to drop the atomic bombs on Japan a hard decision to make?

Did You Know?

• At the 1904 St. Louis World's Fair, there were 142 miles of exhibits in the eight main palaces for visitors to explore.

Chapter Seven

Modern Missouri

After World War II, rapid changes took place in Missouri and the rest of the country. By the end of the war, there were jet planes and rockets that could go into space, television, and computers. But what was new and modern in 1946 is old-fashioned today. What has been Missouri's role in these modern times?

Modern Transportation

Remember reading that crossing Missouri meant a rough-and-tumble ride in a stagecoach or pushing a car out of the mud on a dirt road? Well, what used to take days now takes only hours. And the ride is usually much more comfortable.

Automobiles

The first automobiles appeared in Missouri in 1890. In the beginning, cars and trucks were made one at a time in a garage or a small factory. As the demand for cars and trucks grew, large factories with assembly lines were built. An **assembly line** is a way of making hundreds of cars a day. The car is put together on a moving "belt." People and machines add the parts to the car as it moves past them. Some of these large automobile factories were built in Kansas City and St. Louis. In those cities, there were enough workers to make the cars. There were also railroads to ship the parts in and the finished cars out.

Today, Missouri is second only to Michigan in the number of cars and trucks its factories make. The St. Louis area has auto

The St. Louis skyline reflects the modern, busy city. Yet there is also much history, culture, and entertainment here.

and truck factories in Wentzville, Hazelwood, and Fenton. The Kansas City area has a plant in Claycomo. There is also an assembly plant just across the state line in Kansas where many Missourians work.

Missouri also has many smaller factories across the state that make parts for cars and trucks. These factories make seat covers, plastic lenses for tail lights, fan belts and rubber hoses, and other items. About 31,900 Missourians worked in the auto-making industry in 1999.

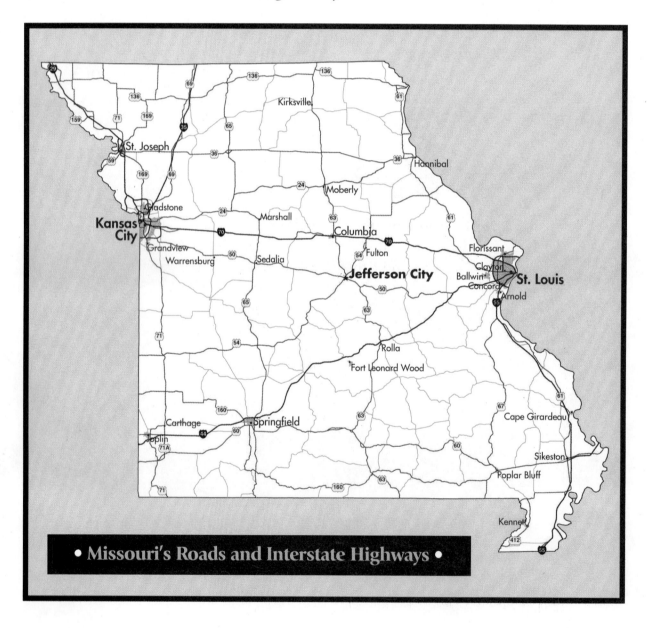

• Missouri's Roads and Interstate Highways •

Missouri's roads have kept up with the increases in cars and trucks. In fact, Missouri has the second-largest system of highways in the country. The state has more than 15,000 miles of road. About 1,200 of those miles are **interstate highways**, which are roads that connect several states. The very first mile of interstate highway in the United States was built in 1956 in St. Charles County, Missouri.

Missouri's fine highways ensure that people and goods travel easily throughout the state. This truck is delivering goods on state highway 79.

Aircraft

Missourians have been flying almost as long as there have been ways to fly. In 1909, the first international air show was held in St. Louis County. Nine airplanes entered. President Theodore Roosevelt attended the show and became the first president to fly in a plane.

St. Louis soon grew to be an important airport and aircraft manufacturing center. James S. McDonnell and two other persons started an airplane factory at the St. Louis airport in 1939. Their company later joined with Douglas Aircraft Company

to become McDonnell-Douglas Aircraft Corporation. The company was one of the largest airplane manufacturers in the world, making both military aircraft and passenger planes. It continues to do so, now as part of the Boeing Corporation. Many smaller factories in Missouri make aircraft parts.

Another famous name in the aircraft industry is William P. Lear, who was born in Hannibal. One of his inventions was a small jet engine for an aircraft he called the LearJet. Many businesses use LearJets today to carry employees from city to city.

Each day, hundreds of planes land and take off from the airports in Kansas City and St. Louis. Commercial airlines also fly to Branson, Cape Girardeau, Columbia, St. Joseph, and Springfield. Many smaller towns have airports where small airplanes can land and take off. Some have paved runways, others are simply grass fields with markings.

Alan Shepard, Jr., the first American to fly into space, blasted off in 1961. He rode aboard a Mercury capsule made by McDonnell-Douglas in St. Louis. The company made all of the Mercury one-person and Gemini two-person spacecraft. It also made major parts of the Apollo spacecraft that went to the moon.

Today, the former McDonnell-Douglas, as part of Boeing, continues to make missiles, satellites, and parts for the space shuttles. It is also helping to design a future space station. But Boeing is not the only company in Missouri involved in space. Some of the earliest rocket motors were made by the Rocketdyne Corporation in Neosho.

At least three Missourians have flown in space. Richard N. Richards of St. Louis was the pilot of a space shuttle flight. Dr. Linda Godwin of Cape Girardeau and Blaine Hammond of Kirkwood have been crew members on shuttle flights.

Railroads and Rapid Transit

Kansas City and St. Louis are the second- and third-largest rail centers in the United States. Major railroads connect the two cities with the rest of the country. Springfield is also an important rail center.

Once, you could travel by train to many places in Missouri. Today airplanes and cars have replaced most of the passenger trains. You can still take an Amtrak train between St. Louis and Kansas City, across northern Missouri between Kansas City and Chicago, or through southeast Missouri from St. Louis to Little Rock, Arkansas. The trains stop in several Missouri towns along the way.

Missouri's large cities and many of its smaller ones used to have electric-powered streetcars. **Streetcars** carried many people and ran along rails laid in the street. Cars and buses have replaced the streetcars. But as roads become more crowded, cities are again looking at streetcars and light rail lines as a way to help people travel in urban areas. Light rail lines are like streetcars, but their tracks are usually separate from the roadway. They can accelerate quickly and travel at high speeds. St. Louis already has a light rail line called MetroLink, and Kansas City is planning a light rail line.

This Amtrak train is traveling between St. Louis and Kansas City. It stops in Washington to pick up passengers.

Towns that could not be reached by railroad used to be connected by bus lines. Several bus companies used to run in Missouri. But as more people started to own cars of their own, fewer rode the buses. Today, only a few bus lines cross Missouri, although tour buses still travel to tourist spots.

Missouri is a leading manufacturer of rail equipment. Warning lights and other devices that help make the railroads safer are made in Kansas City. Rail cars to haul grain and dry chemicals are made in St. Charles and Cape Girardeau.

River Travel

One of the things that attracted early traders and settlers to Missouri was its many rivers. French fur trappers in their pirogues (pronounced "Pih Roags"), rivermen with their keelboats, and pilots of steam-driven paddle wheelers—all have hauled freight up and down the state's rivers.

Today, strings of many barges tied together are pushed up the Mississippi and Missouri rivers by towboats. A **barge** is a

These barges are tied up on the Mississippi River at New Madrid. Barges usually carry heavy, bulky goods.

large flat-bottomed boat used on rivers and canals to carry goods. The barges are loaded with coal, grain, chemicals, and fuels at docks called **terminals**. The cargoes are shipped upstream or downstream to other terminals.

Few people travel on the river anymore. There are some cruise boats, such as the *Delta Queen* and the *Mississippi Queen*, that carry passengers on vacations up and down the rivers. Missouri's river towns are regular stops for these boats.

To slow the Mississippi River down and make it deep enough for boats, **dams** (barriers across the river) have been built. There are 26 dams on the Mississippi between St. Louis and Minneapolis, Minnesota. Barges and other boats cannot go through or over the dams, so locks are built beside the dams. The **locks** have gates on each end to let the water in or out. The water on the upstream side of the dam is higher than on the downstream side. Once a boat is in the lock, the water level is raised or lowered, depending on which direction the barge or other boat is going.

Modern steamboats, like the Delta Queen, *offer passengers the opportunity to discover Mark Twain's America and to explore the river towns and cities. The oldest overnight paddle wheeler, the* Delta Queen, *is a National Historic Landmark.*

The lock and dam at Saverton is #22 of 26 dams on the upper Mississippi River. These dams make sure the river is deep enough for safe boating.

You can see locks and dams near Canton, Clarksville, Saverton, St. Louis, Taylor, West Alton, and Winfield. There are also dams on the Missouri River. But they are much farther upstream and are used for flood control. They do not have locks.

Modern Technology

Your grandparents probably read a comic strip called "Dick Tracy." It was about a police officer who wore a television set the size of a watch on his wrist. He used it to talk with other police officers. It was all make-believe. Your grandparents probably never thought that some day people really would wear television sets on their wrists. **Technology**—applying science to our everyday lives—has come a long way!

Communications

In Chapter 6 you read about radio. That is just one of the ways Missourians can communicate.

Television

Television was invented before World War II. But only a few people had television sets then. There weren't any "real" television stations until after the war. Missouri's first television station was KSD-TV (now KSDK-TV) in St. Louis, which went on the air in 1947. By 1999, there were 29 television stations in Missouri (along with 196 radio stations).

Today there are television sets small enough to carry in our pockets or so large that the screen covers an entire wall. Your parents may remember when shows were in black and white and there were only 3 or 4 channels to watch. Today, the shows are in color and you can choose from more than 100 channels.

Newspapers

One of the reasons we watch television or listen to the radio is to learn about the news. Another way is to read the newspaper. There were 358 newspapers in Missouri in 1999, including 46 daily newspapers. Most medium-sized or larger towns have a local newspaper, usually printed once a week.

Missouri's first newspaper was the *Missouri Gazette*. It was first **published** (printed) in St. Louis in 1808. Another early newspaper was the *Missouri Intelligencer and Boon's Lick Advertiser*. It was first published in Franklin in 1819.

Many of the early immigrants to Missouri did not speak English when they arrived. To help them, newspapers were published in their native languages. And because few newspapers carried news about blacks—unless they were famous or the news also involved a white person—several black newspapers were started. Among the first were the *St. Louis Argus* in 1912, the *Kansas City Call* in 1919, and the *St. Louis American* in 1928.

Publishing

Newspapers are just one of the things printed in Missouri. Several companies publish books, including textbooks for schools. Several magazines are published in Missouri, including *The Sporting News*, a weekly publication about sports that is sent all around the country.

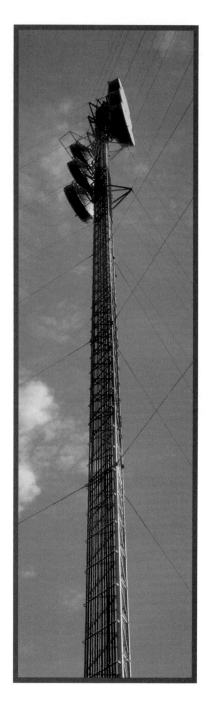

Microwave towers such as this one in Gentry County, relay voice, printed, graphic, photographic, and video communications.

Did you receive a card on your last birthday? Chances are good that it was printed in Kansas City. That is the home of Hallmark Cards, the world's largest greeting card company.

Computers

Your school probably has computers. You might even have a computer at home. Today, they are a part of our everyday lives. But it was not long ago that computers were only used by scientists and big businesses.

Before World War II, scientists began experimenting with computers that used electronic parts. Some of the first electronic computers were so big that they weighed 30 tons and took up the whole basement in a building. All they could do was arithmetic—but they did that very quickly!

With the invention of the Internet, personal computers have become an important new way to communicate and learn.

The large electronic parts have been replaced with computer chips. Computer chips as small as the head of a pin can do as much work as that basement-size computer did 50 years ago. The chips are cut from wafers made out of silicon, a mineral found in the earth. One of the world's largest manufacturers of silicon wafers is found in O'Fallon.

Computers are used not only for keeping records, helping with your homework, or creating art, but also for communicating. One way is through **e-mail**, which is like writing a letter. But instead of mailing it in an envelope, you send it electronically. It reaches its destination almost immediately.

Another way is through the Internet, or World Wide Web. Individuals, businesses, organizations, and maybe even your school have created Web pages or sites containing information or entertainment. If you have a computer, you can see these Web sites or create your own Web page.

Often, many computers are linked in a **network** that lets users share the same **software** (the instructions that tell the computer what to do). The computers in your school may be part of a network.

Health Care

When we think of all the modern inventions that make our lives better, we sometimes forget the changes in medicine and health care that have improved our lives.

When you were a baby, your parents took you to the doctor to receive vaccinations. A **vaccine** protects us from such diseases as German measles, whooping cough, and tetanus. But when your great-grandparents were children, there were no vaccines for some diseases.

Today, drugs make it possible to fight diseases and medical problems like cancer, heart disease, and mental illness. New tools let doctors see inside our bodies and take pictures to tell them if anything is wrong. Doctors can now make minor repairs without a major operation. And they can replace damaged organs with transplanted donor organs.

Doctors learn about new drugs, new tools, and new methods at medical school. Missouri has four medical schools: the University of Missouri in Columbia, Washington University in St. Louis, St. Louis University, and the School of Osteopathy in

Washington University School of Medicine in St. Louis was founded in 1891. It has trained over 6,000 physicians.

Hallmark

The chances are good that the cards you send people for their birthdays were designed and printed by Hallmark, a Kansas City company that is the world's largest greeting card manufacturer. Each day, Hallmark prints 11 million cards in more than 20 languages for sale around the world. But Hallmark does more than sell greeting cards. It also sells wrapping paper, Christmas ornaments, ribbons and bows, books, puzzles, and Crayola crayons. It also sponsors television shows.

Joyce C. Hall turned $3,500 he had earned during high school into the largest greeting card company in the world.

The company was started by Joyce C. Hall. Mr. Hall was a Nebraskan who came to Kansas City in 1910 at age 18 to start

a picture-postcard business. He was later joined by his brothers Rollie and William. They called their company Hall Brothers. In 1912, they started selling greeting cards. They started printing their own cards in 1914.

The company became the largest greeting card company because the Hall brothers seemed to know what type of cards people were going to want. They also advertised their cards in magazines and on the radio—something other card markers did not do. In 1936, the Hall brothers set up a counter in a store where people could see all the cards and serve themselves. Before then, greeting cards were usually kept under a counter in the store. You had to tell the clerk what kind of card you wanted.

The company's slogan, "When you care enough to send the very best," was first used in 1944. In 1954, the company changed its name to Hallmark, a name it had been using on its cards since 1921. Today, you can visit Hallmark's Crown Center in downtown Kansas City. It has three floors of shops—including a Hallmark card store—a hotel, and a Halls department store. At the Hallmark Visitor Center, you can learn about the company's history and how greeting cards are made.

Kansas City's Crown Center is home to shopping, dining, entertainment, office space, living space, and attractions. It is also the international headquarters of Hallmark Cards, Inc.

Kirksville. There are also schools in Missouri that teach pharmacists (druggists), dentists, eye doctors, and chiropractors. Many other schools train nurses and other healthcare workers.

Other people have studied ways to make our lives safer. That is why we have seat belts to use when we ride in a car and helmets to wear when we ride our bicycles. Technology has certainly helped Missourians live healthier, longer lives.

Modern Manufacturing

Cars and airplanes are not the only things Missouri manufactures. Look around your house. Almost everything you see could have been made in Missouri. That includes the toaster on the kitchen counter, the hangers in your closet, and even the bathtub in your bathroom.

The first factories in Missouri made goods out of the raw materials found in the state: wood, iron (which was made into steel), lead, leather, cotton, and wool. Today, you can find factories that

The home office of Anheuser-Busch, the world's largest brewer, is in St. Louis. These buildings are part of the St. Louis brewery.

make wooden broom handles in Bernie and steel anchors for telephone poles in Centralia. Lead batteries are made in Joplin and leather footballs in Licking. A factory in Jefferson City makes cotton balls and one in Bourbon makes wool stocking caps.

Missouri also has factories that make unusual products. In Linn, you can find a cuestick factory. In Dexter, a company still makes straw hats. Disposable diapers are made in a large plant in Jackson. Kitty litter is made by a factory at Bloomfield.

At one time, Missouri was the country's leading producer of shoes. There were shoe factories all over the state. Most of those shoe factories have moved to other countries.

Missouri has long been a leading garment-making state. Just about every county in the state has a factory making some kind of clothing. Gloves are made in Brunswick, and raincoats in Iberia. A factory makes overalls in Hermitage. Appleton City has a factory that makes uniforms. Most of these factories are small and might employ 200 or fewer workers. But they are very important to a small town's economy.

New technologies and new inventions need factories. There are many small factories in Missouri that make computer equipment, medical equipment, medicines, plastics, electrical gear, tools, robots, and farm chemicals.

Many of the machines in newer factories use robots and computers and need skilled employees to make them work. To train workers for these new technologies, there are trade schools and special classes in high schools in many school districts.

Modern Agriculture

Missouri farmers have benefited from new farming methods and better equipment. A modern farmer produces enough food to feed 11 other people. Farm products from Missouri feed people all over the world.

Soybeans, corn, and hay are the state's biggest crops. About one-third of the money Missouri farmers make each year is from soybeans. Winter wheat, cotton, sorghum, and rice are also important crops. Missouri ranks among the top producers of beef

Soybeans, seen growing here in Pemiscot County in the Bootheel, are one of Missouri's most important crops.

cattle and hogs. The state is still a major producer of mules and horses. Large numbers of turkeys and chickens are raised here.

New Machinery and Methods

The biggest changes in agriculture since World War II have been in machinery and chemicals. There were tractors before the war. But many farmers still used horses and mules and did many chores by hand. After the war, most farmers bought tractors and other machines to do the work. Today, farmers produce more crops with fewer people.

One example of how machinery has replaced people is the cotton picker. This machine is a type of tractor with parts on the front that can cleanly pull the cotton bolls (the white, fluffy part) from the plants. One cotton picker machine can do the work that hundreds of people used to do by hand.

Agricultural colleges like the University of Missouri also help farmers. Research has provided better seeds, better fertilizers, better chemicals to control bugs and weeds, and better farming methods. Research at the University and at companies like Monsanto in St. Louis has also helped farmers raise better animals. Beef cattle now have less fat in their meat, dairy cows give more milk, chickens lay more eggs, and turkeys are larger. We sometimes call agricultural research *biotech research* because it combines biology and technology.

Just as people are living healthier lives because of modern medicine, modern animal medicine has meant healthier animals. Students from all over the country come to the University of Missouri School of Veterinary Medicine in Columbia to learn to become **veterinarians**, doctors who care for farm animals and our pets.

Farm-Related Businesses

Not everyone who makes a living in agriculture is a farmer. For instance, there are seed and tractor salespeople, workers at grain elevators, employees at fertilizer and chemical plants, and workers at stockyards.

Other people make a living turning farm products into the food we buy at the store. Much of

the flour for our bread, the grains for our breakfast cereals, and the corn syrup for our soft drinks are made in Kansas City and St. Joseph. Your Thanksgiving turkey probably came from a processing plant in the town of California. Marshall has a plant that produces frozen chicken dinners. Excelsior Springs has a factory that turns wheat and eggs into pasta.

Missouri has become famous for its beer and wines. Anheuser-Busch, the world's largest beer brewer, has its headquarters and one of its breweries in St. Louis. Grapes for wine are grown in several parts of the state, but mostly along the Missouri River between Rocheport and Augusta.

Other Types of Workers

Many Missourians do not work in factories or in agriculture. Some are **service workers**, people who do something for others. In your school, service workers include the people who clean the rooms and floors, the people who cook the meals, and the people who work in the office answering the telephone and keeping the records. Other examples of service workers include bus drivers, delivery people, repair people, people who install telephones, tour guides, and the people who run the rides at the amusement park.

This tour guide (a service worker) is describing the vegetable garden at Watkins Woolen Mill State Historic Site to two visitors.

People who work in stores are called **retail workers**. Some examples are the workers who check your groceries, the people who put the goods on the shelves, and the clerks who help you try on new shoes. The person who sells you popcorn at the movies and the person your parents buy a new car from are retail workers.

Some Missourians are doctors or lawyers or work in jobs that require a college education. These workers are called **professionals**. Your teacher is a professional. He or she had to go to college to learn how to be a teacher. Other professionals include nurses, librarians, school principals, bankers, and scientists.

Tourism

One of the most important parts of Missouri's economy is something that does not make anything, grow anything, or mine anything. **Tourism** is an industry that depends on people

Tourists come to Missouri to enjoy the many attractions in the state. These tourists are walking the streets of Hannibal's Historic District.

visiting an area for fun. The tourism industry employs hundreds of thousands of Missourians.

More than a million people visit Missouri each year. They come here to see the museums, the zoos, the amusement parks, and the sporting events. They come here to fish, swim, and boat in our lakes and rivers. They come to go to the state and county fairs and to enjoy concerts, plays, and dancing. They come to hike and bike on our trails, to camp in our parks, and to just look at the scenery.

Tourists spend billions of dollars each year in Missouri. They stay at motels, buy tickets to shows and games, eat at restaurants, buy bait for fishing, and fill up at gas stations.

Daniel Boone's home near Defiance is a popular tourist destination.

Summary

In this chapter, you learned that Missouri has seen many changes since World War II, including many new inventions and new technologies. These have helped make life better for Missourians. You also learned that Missouri is a leading producer of automobiles and trucks and airplanes. They are made in large factories that employ thousands of people. There are many smaller factories in Missouri as well, producing things we use every day.

Missouri is also a leading agricultural state. Modern machines and methods have helped farmers grow more food with fewer workers. Many nonfarmers work in agriculture-related jobs, turning farm products into the food we buy in the grocery store.

Tourism is also an important industry in Missouri. The millions of people who visit Missouri every year spend a lot of money and provide jobs for thousands of workers.

Chapter • Review

Reviewing Vocabulary

assembly lines

e-mail

interstate highways

locks

published

service workers

vaccines

veterinarian

On a sheet of paper, write the numbers 1 to 8. Beside each number, write the word or phrase from the list above that best completes the sentence.

1. _____ help protect us from some diseases.
2. Boats must use _____ to get around dams on the rivers.
3. If an animal is sick or injured, you would take it to a _____.
4. Cars and trucks are put together on _____.
5. We use _____ to send messages by computer.
6. _____ do things for other people.
7. _____ are roads that connect several states.
8. When a newspaper or book is printed, we say it has been _____.

Reviewing Facts

1. Name four ways we can travel in Missouri.
2. Why were auto and truck factories located in Missouri?
3. What role have Missourians played in exploring space?
4. What types of goods do barges carry?
5. Why were dams built on Missouri's rivers?
6. What was Missouri's first newspaper?
7. Name three ways we can use computers.
8. What are the major crops grown in Missouri today?
9. Name three reasons why tourists come to Missouri.

Using What You've Learned

1. Make a list of all the companies in your community or neighborhood. You can get this information from the chamber of commerce, the telephone book, or in books at the library. Use this information to make a list of all the goods that are made in your community.
2. Make a list of the types of workers who can be found at your school.

Building Skills

1. Why is it important for someone living in modern Missouri to stay in school and learn as much as possible?
2. Have the changes brought about by television and the automobile been good or bad for your community?

Did You Know?

- The Atlas Portland Cement Company provided cement for the Panama Canal.
- The largest employer in Missouri is the Boeing Co. in St. Louis.

Chapter Eight

The Struggles for Freedom

Captain Wendell Oliver Pruitt was a fighter pilot in World War II. During the war, he shot down 11 enemy airplanes. For that he received the Distinguished Flying Cross, one of the highest honors a pilot can earn. When he returned to this country and his hometown of St. Louis, Captain Pruitt told a newspaper reporter his hopes for the future. "I hope we will find the 'Four Freedoms' realized when we return," he said.

What did Captain Pruitt mean? To most Americans, the war was about preserving what President Franklin Roosevelt had said were the Four Freedoms. These were: the freedom of expression (speaking and writing our thoughts, opinions, and ideas), the freedom of worship, the freedom from want (another way of saying poverty), and the freedom from fear.

But for some Americans, these freedoms were little more than hopes. Growing up in Missouri, Captain Pruitt was one of those for whom the Four Freedoms were just a dream. That was because Captain Pruitt was an African American.

Making Freedom Real

The struggle by African Americans to win basic freedoms and rights began at the end of the Civil War. Along with giving them their freedom from slavery, the Civil War gave many African Americans a sense of being more than just someone's property. By fighting in the war, many African Americans believed that they had contributed to the rebirth of the nation and that they had a right to share in its future.

Captain Wendell Pruitt was a member of the famous Tuskegee Airmen, a group of black fighter pilots.

Former slaves line up to receive help from the Freedmen's Bureau.

Reconstruction

You will remember that the years right after the Civil War are known as *Reconstruction*. During this time, the nation had to reconstuct the things destroyed in the war. It also had to reconstruct the feelings of being a united country.

The newly freed slaves found that life after slavery was little better than before. In some ways it was worse. Many of them no longer had a place to live or work. Many remained on the farms where they had been slaves, working for little or no wages. Others moved to the towns and cities. There they found only low-paying jobs as servants or laborers, a shortage of housing, and discrimination. **Discrimination** is unequal and unfair treatment that denies people their rights because of their race, sex, religion, or any other reason. Much discrimination is rooted in **racism**, a belief that one's own race is better than all others.

The federal government tried to help. It had started the **Freedmen's Bureau** in 1865. This organization provided food, clothing, medical care, and other help to former slaves. In Missouri, it also served as a go-between for black laborers and

James Milton Turner

James Milton Turner was born a slave on a St. Louis County farm on May 16, 1839. His father was a skilled horse doctor who was able to buy his family's freedom when young Milton (as he was called) was 4 years old. Turner went to secret schools in St. Louis and enrolled at Oberlin College in Ohio at age 14. He returned to Missouri after the Civil War, after serving in the Union army.

In 1865, Turner joined the Missouri Equal Rights League. He was soon elected its secretary. This job took him all around the state as he sought support for voting rights for black Missourians. Turner was a skilled speaker who could excite his audiences with his words and his style.

Turner also worked as a teacher at the first black public schools in Kansas City and Boonville. He was hired by the Freedmen's Bureau and the American Missionary Association to set up schools for black children all around Missouri. In one year, he helped to build 7 new school buildings and to open 32 schools altogether.

In 1871, President U.S. Grant appointed Turner ambassador to Liberia, an African colony set up by former American slaves. He served in that post until 1878, when he returned to Missouri. Turner continued to work for equal rights for African Americans. He led efforts to integrate Missouri's schools, arguing that separate schools for black and white children were unconstitutional. When the number of lynchings grew in the 1890s, Turner and other black leaders wrote an appeal to all Americans, calling for an end to the violence.

Turner died on November 1, 1915, in Ardmore, Oklahoma, when a building he was in collapsed after an explosion. His body was brought back to St. Louis for the largest funeral for a black resident the city had ever seen. James Milton Turner is buried in a cemetery not far from his birthplace.

James Milton Turner was one of Missouri's first civil rights leaders. He worked tirelessly to establish schools for black children.

One important task of the Freedmen's Bureau was to establish schools for the former slaves and their children. Before the Civil War, it was illegal to teach slaves to read and write.

former slave owners who could no longer farm without slave labor. The Freedmen's Bureau, largely through the efforts of James Milton Turner, helped start schools for the former slaves and their children.

Meanwhile, African Americans in Missouri were helping themselves. After the war, they organized the Missouri Equal Rights League to work for **suffrage** (the right to vote). When the Fifteenth Amendment to the U.S. Constitution was finally ratified in 1870, African-American men gained the right to vote.

Many African-American soldiers from Missouri had learned to read and write while in the army. They knew how important education was. So, they donated money in 1866 to start Lincoln Institute in Jefferson City to train African-American teachers. Today, it is Lincoln University.

Separate But Equal

Reconstruction in Missouri ended in 1876 when the politicians who favored it were voted out of office. The new politicians began passing laws that kept blacks from using the same buildings and public services as whites. These laws came to be known as **Jim Crow laws**. The courts ruled against efforts to end this segregation. In one decision, the U.S. Supreme Court ruled that "separate but equal" was all right.

But separate schools for African-American children were rarely equal to the schools for white children. Many did not have chalkboards. Some schools had leaky roofs. Others did not have drinking water nearby. Students often had to sit on benches instead of at desks. Some towns could not afford both black and white high schools. So black students had to travel many miles to a town that had a school for them.

The right to vote and the chance to get an education gave African Americans new power. Some people did not want African Americans to have this power. These people began harassing (bothering) African Americans—trying to keep them from voting, from living in their towns, from going to school, or from starting businesses. One terrible way of harassing and

Lincoln University in Jefferson City was founded to educate the freed slaves. Today it serves students of many social, economic, educational, and cultural backgrounds.

scaring people was **lynching**, which is mob murder usually by hanging. Most of the victims were black men.

Segregated Cities

As more and more African Americans moved to the cities, the small areas of the cities where they were allowed to live became more and more crowded. Sometimes two or three families lived

When this photograph was taken in 1908, many cities were segregated. These children lived in a black area of St. Louis.

in a one-room or two-room apartment. Several families living in a building usually had to share one bathroom. These dirty, crowded areas are called **slums** and still exist in many cities.

Blacks had few chances for education beyond grade school or high school. They could not get the education or training needed for better jobs. White employers often would not hire African Americans or would only hire them for low-paying jobs. Low wages meant little money for decent housing, proper health care, or healthy diets.

Even if a black family saved its money and could afford a nice house, the family found it difficult to buy one. White real estate agents would not sell to them. And whites would not let blacks move into their neighborhoods.

Segregation and discrimination led blacks to start organizations like the Urban League and the National Association for the Advancement of Colored People (NAACP). Because labor unions would not admit them, African Americans formed their own. (A **labor union** is an organization of workers formed to improve wages and working conditions.) The largest black labor union represented railroad porters. African-American newspapers also became important in this period. They urged their readers to help each other and to rely on their own skills and hard work to get ahead.

World War I

When the United States entered World War I, many African-American men volunteered for the armed forces. They often had a hard time being accepted. Usually they worked only as cooks or truck drivers. Few were actually allowed to fight.

Back home, so many white men had joined the armed forces that factories were short of workers. They had to hire African-American men. That led to an **exodus** (departure) of black families from farms in the South to factory cities in the North. Many found jobs in the factories of Kansas City and St. Louis. By 1920, there were fewer than 4,000 African-American farmers remaining in Missouri.

The taste of better-paying jobs and the idea that having fought for the United States should mean better treatment made African Americans all the more determined to gain equal

When World War I began, many African Americans left the South for jobs in the factories and cities of the North. This exodus is sometimes called the "Great Migration."

rights. More began running for political office. In 1920, Walthall Moore of St. Louis became the first African American elected to the Missouri General Assembly. He had the help of the Citizens Liberty League, one of the many African-American political groups formed after World War I.

Ku Klux Klan

This renewed struggle for equal rights by African Americans was seen as a threat by some whites. They sometimes formed groups with others who thought the same way. Some of these groups were peaceful, others were violent and hateful.

One hate group was the **Ku Klux Klan** (KKK), a group that had been around since right after the Civil War. It was originally a social club for former Confederate soldiers. But by the

This Ku Klux Klan march took place in Washington, D.C., in 1926.

1920s, the KKK was made up of people who blamed their troubles on blacks, Catholics, Jews, and other people they did not understand.

In Missouri, the KKK took part in lynchings. It burned churches and businesses belonging to African Americans and Jews. It also tried to prevent African Americans and Catholics from voting or running for office. Sometimes, it tried to scare people by wearing hoods and burning crosses.

Most Missourians wanted nothing to do with the KKK. They pushed for the arrest of KKK members who broke the law. When KKK members tried to run for political office, they were usually defeated. In Missouri, support for the KKK dried up.

African Americans and the Depression

Few Americans escaped the hardships of the Great Depression. But blacks were especially hard hit because most of them were already so poor. As factories and businesses closed, jobs became harder and harder to find. African-American workers were usually the last hired and first fired. Many lost their jobs to white workers.

Groups like the Urban League in Kansas City started programs to teach African-American workers job skills. Many African Americans in Missouri joined New Deal programs like the Civilian Conservation Corps, helping to build state parks.

Perhaps the hardest hit of all by the Depression were black farm workers. Most were tenant farmers or *sharecroppers* who worked for a share of the crops they grew for the landowners. The sharecroppers, both black and white, were very poor. The amount of money a sharecropper made in one year would not even buy a pair of basketball shoes today. Sharecropper

The Thunderbird Lodge at Washington State Park. The lodge was built by African-American members of the Civilian Conservation Corps during the Great Depression.

families lived in shacks and had few new clothes. Some had no shoes or winter coats for their children.

As the Depression became worse, conditions for farmers grew worse. Many landowners in southeast Missouri evicted their sharecroppers. (To **evict** is to force a person off the land.) The evicted families faced death from starvation.

Owen Whitfield, an African-American minister from the Bootheel, organized a march of the sharecroppers along the Bootheel highways. The sharecroppers and their families carried all of their possessions on their backs or in carts. They slept along the roadsides. One newspaper called them "Missouri's refugees." This nonviolent **Sharecroppers Rebellion** led the federal government to step in and help Missouri's sharecroppers and other farmers.

Black Americans and World War II

The Depression ended with the coming of World War II. Again, African-American Missourians answered the call to duty. They were placed in all-black units and used mostly as cooks, hospital workers, or supply clerks. Captain Wendell Pruitt was one exception. Pruitt was a member of the famous Tuskegee Airmen, a group of black fighter pilots.

Left: In January 1939, evicted Bootheel sharecroppers camped along two state highways to protest their situation.

With so many white men away at war, factories again had to hire black men and black and white women to fill the jobs. Still more black families moved from the South to the North and the West to fill these jobs.

Missourian Thomas Hart Benton painted this picture of an African-American G.I. (regular soldier).

This photograph of a black teacher and her students was taken in the 1930s. Elementary schools at that time were segregated.

The Civil Rights Movement

In World War II, black Americans fought and died around the world for freedoms they did not have at home. They were determined not to let things go back to the way they were.

Although Captain Pruitt did not live to see it happen, things started to change after World War II. Slowly, with help from organizations like the NAACP, African Americans began breaking down the color barriers. In 1948, Harry S Truman, the president from Missouri, ordered an end to segregation and discrimination in the armed forces.

Changes were slowly taking place in other parts of society. The courts played a major role in those changes.

Integrating the Schools

The first African-American student to try to enter the University of Missouri was Lloyd Gaines in 1936. He was a Lincoln

University graduate who wanted to be a lawyer. But the University of Missouri's law school did not admit African Americans. Gaines took the matter to court. The U.S. Supreme Court eventually said Missouri had to either allow him into the University's law school or provide a black law school. Rather than allow African-American students into the University, the state opened a separate law school. In 1939, Lucille Bluford tried to enter the University's journalism school. Again, the state chose to open a separate journalism school for African Americans. But in 1950, four Lincoln University students applied to the University. A judge in Jefferson City ordered the University of Missouri to admit African-American students.

Catholic elementary and high schools in Missouri were integrated in 1947. (**Integration** is the process of bringing different groups or races into society as equals.) But the state's public elementary and high schools were not officially integrated until 1956. They were integrated only after the courts ordered them to do so.

The deciding case involved a young girl named Linda Brown who lived in Topeka, Kansas. She wanted to go to the school in her neighborhood, but it did not allow African Americans. Her family sued the local school board. The case, known as *Brown vs. Board of Education*, went all the way to the U.S. Supreme Court. In 1954, the Supreme Court ruled that "separate but equal" was really "unequal." One year later, the Court ordered school boards to integrate their schools.

When the schools were integrated, students of all races went to school together.

Public schools in Kansas City and St. Louis were officially integrated. But because the neighborhoods in those cities were still segregated, so were the schools. The courts ordered that **busing** be used to integrate the schools. African-American students were sent by buses to all-white schools, and white students were sent by buses to all-black schools.

Protests and Demonstrations

People in Missouri—both black and white—protested against the state's Jim Crow laws. One method of protest was a **boycott**, where people refuse to do business with a certain store or restaurant or company. Another form of protest was the **sit-in**, where people went into a building such as a restaurant and refused to leave until they were served or forced to leave. One sit-in took place in Jefferson City. The high school football team went to a local restaurant after a game. The owner refused to serve the African-American players. The white players left without eating or paying for the food they had ordered. Then they blocked the front door until the owner changed his mind and served the African-American players.

Dr. Martin Luther King, Jr., was a leader of the civil rights movement. He called for nonviolent protests all across the nation. There were sit-ins at restaurants, on buses, at hotels, and in schools. There were marches and demonstrations. The marchers usually remained peaceful, but sometimes the police reacted violently. The nonviolent protests were very effective. In 1964 and 1965, Congress passed the **Civil Rights Acts**, which barred discrimination based on race, creed, or color.

Not everyone was satisfied with how quickly—or slowly—changes were taking place. African-American groups that favored stronger actions formed. Some of the actions of these groups were not peaceful. In many cities around the country, there were **riots** (violent, public disorders) because people were angry at the way they were being treated. Missouri escaped these riots until 1968.

Top: These people were protesting against segregation in St. Louis. Above: Dr. Martin Luther King, Jr., was a leader in the civil rights movement.

In April 1968, Dr. King was shot and killed. Schools all around the country closed the next day as a sign of respect. But not the schools in Kansas City. African-American students in Kansas City protested by refusing to go to school. Instead, they marched peacefully to city hall. The police fired tear gas at the students. African Americans were angry over how the students had been treated. That night, they started a riot—breaking windows, throwing rocks at police, burning buildings, and overturning cars. The Highway Patrol and the National Guard had to help the police restore order. Several people were killed, more were injured, and many arrested. Unfortunately, most of the damage was done to black-owned or black-operated businesses.

After Dr. King was killed, there were riots in many cities in the United States. In Kansas City (below), national guardsmen patrolled the streets. In the background, a building burns and a motorist is stopped.

Making Progress

In 1957, the Missouri Human Rights Commission was created. The Commission has worked hard to stop discrimination. It has helped people win their rights in court and has worked for changes in the law. The Commission worked to get the General Assembly to pass laws for fair employment in 1961. The legislature also passed laws for integration of public buildings in 1965 and fair housing in 1972.

African Americans in Missouri also became more involved in politics. Theodore D. McNeal became the first African American elected to the state Senate in 1960. Two years later, DeVerne Lee Calloway of St. Louis became the first African-American woman elected to the state House of Representatives. Gwen Giles of St. Louis became the first African-American woman elected to the state Senate in 1978. The first African-American Missourian elected to Congress was William Clay of St. Louis in 1968.

African Americans were also making gains in other areas of society. In 1974, Betty Adams of Jefferson City was named director of the Missouri Department of Labor and Management Relations. She was the first African American—and the first woman—to be named the head of a state government department. In 1991, Clarence Harmon became the first African-American chief of police in St. Louis and later was elected mayor.

In business, Louis W. Smith rose to be president of the Kansas City division of Allied Signal Aerospace Co. Reginald Smith was named president of United Missouri Mortgage Company in Kansas City. In education, Marguerite Ross Barnett was appointed the head of the University of Missouri's St. Louis campus in 1986.

Debbye Turner is another African American who became famous in 1990. She was the first Missourian to be selected Miss America. Hal McRae, long a favorite of fans of the Kansas City Royals baseball team, was named the team's manager in 1991. He was the first African American to head a professional sports team in Missouri that included both black and white players.

*Top: In 1960, Theodore McNeal became the first African American elected to the Missouri Senate. **Above:** In 1962, DeVerne Lee Calloway became the first African-American woman elected to the Missouri House of Representatives.*

Mellcene Thurman Smith (far left) and Sarah Lucille Turner (left) were the first women elected to the Missouri House of Representatives. Mary Gant (below) was the first woman elected to the Missouri Senate. Many women have served in the General Assembly since then.

Women's Rights

Women of all colors were also struggling to gain equal rights. The fight for equal rights for women started soon after the Civil War. When Missouri became a state, only white men could vote or hold elected office. After the Civil War, the Fifteenth Amendment gave African-American men the right to vote. Women asked the state legislature for the same right, but they were told no.

In 1914, the question of women's suffrage was put to all the voters in the state. But, maybe because only men could vote, the measure lost. Two years later, when the Democratic party held its national convention in St. Louis, 7,000 women marched outside the convention hall asking for the right to vote.

In 1917, Congress approved the Nineteenth Amendment giving all American women the right to vote. Missouri was one of the first states to ratify it. It became law in 1919. Two years later, Mellcene Thurman Smith of St. Louis and Sarah Lucille Turner of Kansas City became the first women elected to the Missouri House of Representatives. The first woman senator was Mary Gant of Kansas City, elected in 1972. The first Missouri woman elected to Congress was Leonor K. Sullivan of St. Louis, elected in 1951.

The Struggle Continues

When immigrants from non-English-speaking European countries started coming to Missouri in the 1800s, they often ran into discrimination. That was because their languages and customs were different from the Missourians already living here. When Mormons tried to settle in northwest Missouri in the early 1800s, they were driven out by people who did not understand the Mormons' religious beliefs.

Today, new immigrants from Asia, Latin America, and other parts of the world arrive in Missouri every day. Many do not speak English, and they have customs different from ours. They too sometimes face discrimination. But as people learn more about them—just as they learned more about the Mormons, the European immigrants, and the African Americans—they are increasingly welcomed as Missourians.

Summary

In this chapter, you learned that the struggle for real freedom for Missouri's African Americans and for women has been a long and hard one. After the Civil War, many of the freed slaves moved to urban areas, where most African-American Missourians live today. They found poor living conditions, low-paying jobs, and discrimination. They also faced racism. Sometimes the racism took a violent form.

By demonstrating their willingness to die for freedom, not only at home but also in two world wars, black Americans convinced many white Americans to join in their fight. Through court decisions and nonviolent protests, they brought about many changes.

The Reorganized Church of Jesus Christ of Latter Day Saints (RLDS) came into being in the 1850s. Since 1920, the official headquarters of the church has been in Independence. The Temple was completed in 1993.

Chapter • Review

Reviewing Vocabulary

discrimination
evicted
exodus
lynching
racism
sit-in
suffrage

On a sheet of paper, write the numbers 1 to 7. Beside each number, write the word from the list above that best completes the sentence.

1. A _____ occurs when a mob kills a person, usually by hanging.
2. The right to vote is called _____.
3. The movement of black families from the South to northern cities is sometimes called an _____.
4. People forced off a farm or out of an apartment are _____.
5. A _____ is a type of nonviolent protest where people enter a building and refuse to leave.
6. _____ is the belief that one's own race is superior to all others.
7. Unfair treatment that denies people their rights is _____.

Reviewing Facts

1. What was the purpose of the Freedmen's Bureau?
2. What was the name given to the laws in Missouri that barred African Americans from using the same buildings and facilities as whites?
3. Why did African Americans have to form their own labor unions?
4. Why did many African-American families move from the southern farms to the northern and western cities?
5. What was the Ku Klux Klan?
6. What event brought attention to the problems of sharecroppers during the Great Depression?
7. What method was used in Kansas City and St. Louis to integrate the public schools?
8. Who was Dr. Martin Luther King, Jr.?
9. When did women receive the right to vote?

Using What You've Learned

1. Explain the "separate-but-equal" policy.
2. In what ways did people work against segregation, racism, and discrimination?

Building Skills

1. Make a list of ways in which people still discriminate against other people. Why do you think they do it?
2. How would you go about protesting a situation that you believed was wrong?

Did You Know?

• President Franklin Roosevelt named two African Americans from Missouri—Dr. William J. Thompkins and Lester A. Walter —to positions in his administration.

Chapter Nine

A Rich Missouri

Missouri is a rich state. That does not mean that we live in mansions and drive fancy cars. Instead, our riches are found in our soil, our forests, our minerals, and our water. But these riches are not endless. It is important that we preserve those riches as we look to the future.

Natural Resources

A **natural resource** is something found in nature and used by people. Many Missourians make a living using our natural resources. Many more Missourians use our natural resources for recreation.

Soil

Missouri's rich soil enables our farmers to grow enough food to feed not only Missourians but also people around the world. The richest soils for farming are found in northern and southeastern Missouri. The soil in the Ozark Highlands and in the western prairie produces the grasses that feed herds of beef and dairy cattle. It also supports forests of tall trees.

You might wonder how plain old dirt can be rich. Soil is made up of rock that has been broken into small pieces. Some of those pieces are so small that they are dust. The rocks are made up of **minerals**, natural resources that are found in the ground. Plants use the minerals for food to grow healthy leaves,

The soil here helps Missouri farmers grow a wide variety of crops. Some of the richest soil is along the Mississippi River.

After crops have been harvested, farmers plow what is left of the plants back into the soil. This returns needed minerals back to the soil.

stems, seeds, and fruit (the part people usually eat). So, a soil made up of the right minerals is called a "rich" soil.

But it is possible to misuse the soil. When plants grow, they take minerals out of the soil. If a farmer grows the same type of plant over and over in the same soil, the minerals are soon gone. The soil is no longer good for growing crops. To prevent this, farmers **rotate** their crops. That is, they plant a different crop every year in each field. Sometimes they plant nothing at all. When the plants die, they are plowed into the soil, adding minerals back to the soil. Sometimes farmers add fertilizers to the soil when certain minerals are missing.

Soil is also misused by erosion. **Erosion** takes place when water washes the soil away or wind blows it away. Besides carrying away the rich soil, erosion ruins streams that are used by fish and other animals. Grass, trees, and other plants prevent erosion by helping rain water soak into the soil gently. They also hold the soil together with their roots.

Forests

Missouri has about 12 million acres of forests. There are several national and state forests in Missouri. Many people hike and camp in them. But most forests are on private property.

There are many different kinds of trees in Missouri. Most of our forests are made up of oak and hickory trees.

Trees are useful for many reasons, including the wood and the nuts they produce. Trees provide shade to cool us. They block the wind to keep us warm. They help prevent erosion, especially along streams and rivers.

Another way trees are useful is in cleaning the air. Like other plants, trees absorb chemicals from the air. Some of the chemicals are harmful to people. In return, trees produce oxygen, which all living creatures need to survive.

Trees can be harmed by air pollution. **Pollution** is caused by substances that make our air and water dirty and unsafe. Chemicals in the air can kill or weaken a tree. Other threats to trees come from insects, diseases, and fires. It is important to be careful with fire when in the woods because it takes many years for a tree to grow.

Sometimes all the trees in a forest are cut down, leaving nothing to protect the soil and destroying the homes and food sources of animals. It is much better to cut down only a few at a time, replacing each harvested tree with a new planting.

Luckily, trees are a renewable natural resource. That is, when a tree dies or is cut down, a new one can be planted in its place.

Minerals

You have read about the importance of lead mining in Missouri's history and its economy. Today, most of the lead comes from the Viburnum Trend. That is a large deposit of lead stretching across Iron and Reynolds counties in southeast Missouri. More than 400,000 tons of lead are mined each year from shafts deep beneath Earth's surface. The state still produces about 80 percent of the world's lead. Most of it is used for batteries.

Often found with the lead ore are two other valuable minerals—silver and zinc. Silver is a valuable metal used to make jewelry, medals, coins, and serving pieces. Zinc is used to coat other metals to prevent rust and corrosion. Zinc is also combined with copper to make brass. Early lead miners in Missouri didn't realize how valuable the zinc was. They used the mine wastes, which contained zinc, to pave roads. When they found out how valuable zinc was, they dug up the roads to remove it.

Another important mining product in Missouri is limestone. It is used to make cement. Sometimes it is used as a building stone. Limestone is dug from a **quarry**, a large hole in the ground or in a hillside. Also dug from quarries are other rocks that are crushed into gravel and used to pave roads and driveways. Fireclay can also be found in Missouri. Fireclay is used to make bricks for ovens where steel or glass is produced. Missouri's mines also produce tiff, or barite, a mineral that is used in making paint and rubber products.

About one-third of Missouri sits on top of a layer of coal. The layer stretches from Jasper County in the southwest to Clark County in the northeast. Much of this coal is just beneath the surface. To reach it, large shovels first remove the top layer of the soil. This is called open-pit or **strip mining**. About 4 million tons of coal are mined in Missouri each year. But Missouri's coal contains a lot of sulfur, which causes air pollution when the coal is burned. Missouri coal is mixed with low-sulfur coal from western states and used by utility companies.

Missouri has only a handful of oil and natural gas wells. It depends on other states for these fuels.

This Iron Mountain mine near Ironton is an underground iron mine. It was abandoned when the iron ore gave out.

Water

Sometimes we forget how important water is. But it is difficult to go even one whole day without water. We drink it, cook with it, and bathe in it. Water has many other uses. In Missouri, businesses need water to produce the products they make. Water is used to make electricity, either by flowing through generators at a dam or by being heated into steam at a generating plant. Farmers use a lot of water, not only for their livestock to drink, but also for their fields. Farmers **irrigate**, or bring water to, their crops to help them grow.

Luckily, Missouri has many sources of water. We have numerous rivers, lakes, and springs that supply some of our needs. Cities and people in rural areas also depend on wells drilled deep into the ground. This water has to be treated to remove harmful chemicals and germs.

Another important use for water in Missouri is recreation. Residents and visitors alike use Missouri's lakes and streams for fishing, boating, swimming, water skiing, canoeing, and sail boating.

Missouri's water resources provide recreation for boating and fishing.

We have to protect our water from pollution. Treatment plants "scrub" the water that drains from our sinks or toilets. Factories also treat their waste water before releasing it. Sometimes people cause pollution when they dump chemicals into the water or onto the ground. From there the chemicals can wash into our rivers and lakes.

Protecting Our Future

Suppose that one night you were thirsty for a drink of milk. You went to the refrigerator, took out the bottle, and poured yourself a glass. But then you forgot to put the milk away. The next morning, the milk would be sour. You wouldn't have any to put on your cereal. You might say it was an *unwise* use of the milk. It is the same for our natural resources. If we use them unwisely today, we will not have any for tomorrow.

Conservation and Recycling

We can conserve our natural resources by remembering the three R's—reduce, reuse, and recycle. Aluminum cans are one of the easiest containers to recycle.

Conservation and recycling are two ways to use our resources wisely. **Conservation** means that we use only what we need so we can save some for the future. You can conserve electricity by turning off lights you are not using and making sure windows are shut when the heat or air conditioning is on in the house. You can conserve water by not letting the water run while brushing your teeth.

Recycling involves reusing what we can. Many communities in Missouri have recycling programs. In some towns, families put their bottles, plastic containers, cans, and newspapers in special containers at a recycling center. The bottles and cans and other recycled items are turned into new items. This conserves raw materials.

You can practice recycling in the classroom too. Instead of throwing papers away, you can save them to use the clean back side. You could also place them in a box to be taken to the recycling center. Can you think of other ways to recycle and conserve?

Alternative Energy

Our cars and trucks run on fuel made from oil. Most of our electricity is made by burning coal or natural gas or by using nuclear energy. The problem is that these fuels produce pollution. To avoid causing pollution, people are using alternative forms of energy, energy from sources that cause less or no pollution. By using alternative forms of energy, we can conserve not only our oil, coal, and natural gas, but also our clean air and water.

There are a number of alternative energy sources that can generate electricity. These include windmills, hydroelectric dams like Bagnell Dam at the Lake of the Ozarks, solar panels, and the steam that comes from hot springs beneath Earth's surface.

Cars and trucks can run on alternative energy sources too. Electric cars are powered by batteries. Cars can also run on gasohol, gasoline that has been blended with alcohol made from corn.

Dams harness the power of flowing water to produce electricity. Bagnell Dam was completed in 1931. Electric service began on Christmas Eve of that year.

Crowder State Park near Trenton features wooded hillsides, deep ravines, and the nearby Thompson River.

Conservation Areas and State Parks

It is the job of the Missouri Department of Conservation to help us conserve wildlife and our flowers, trees, and other plants. To do that, the Department sets limits on hunting and fishing. It wants to make sure there are enough birds, animals, and fish to reproduce.

The Department of Conservation also manages the state forests. It wants to make sure that birds, animals, and fish have places to live and enough food to eat. The department helps farmers and other landowners manage their land. Sometimes, the department buys or is given land that is set aside as a conservation area, a special place where wildlife is protected.

Our state's natural beauty as well as its air, water, and mineral resources are managed by the Department of Natural Resources. This department sets the rules on clean air and water and on mining.

Wild Turkeys and Indiana Brown Bats

When the first European settlers arrived in Missouri, they found an abundance of wild game (animals that could be hunted for food). Hunters did not have to look far to find something to shoot or trap. But as more and more people arrived, more and more animals were killed. After a while, some animals disappeared entirely from Missouri. Among them were the black bear, mountain lion, passenger pigeon, river otter, and wild turkey.

Passenger pigeons once used to darken the sky with their large flocks. They are now *extinct* (no longer existing). But efforts by conservationists (those who want to protect the natural environment) have helped other animals to recover. By trading animals with other states, Missouri has been able to bring turkeys and river otters back to the state.

By stopping the destruction of the areas in which they live, animals like the black bear once again roam Missouri's southern forests. Similar efforts are now underway to save the Indiana brown bat, which is close to being extinct in Missouri. Conservationists are trying to protect the caves where the bats hibernate and raise their young.

The wild turkey has been brought back from the brink of extinction with the help of both conservationists and hunters. Benjamin Franklin favored the wild turkey as the national bird rather than the bald eagle.

The Department of Natural Resources also manages our state parks and historic sites. There are nearly 50 state parks in Missouri. They range in size from Big Lake State Park's 111 acres to Lake of the Ozarks State Park's 17,000 acres. And the Katy Trail State Park may be only 100 feet wide in most places, but it is 232 miles long!

Some of the parks preserve special features. The bones of prehistoric elephants can be seen at Mastodon State Park near Imperial. Near Lebanon, you can see the spring at Bennett Spring State Park. There are also the rock bridge at Rock Bridge State Park near Columbia and the shut-ins at Johnson Shut-Ins State Park near Middlebrook. A *shut-in* is a section of a stream where rock formations "shut in" the water and cause rapids, waterfalls, and pools. The rocks are usually granite and have been worn smooth by the rushing water.

At Johnson's Shut-ins State Park near Middlebrook, the Black River has found a natural route through the granite rocks. The water has eroded the rocks to form a series of canyonlike gorges.

Preserving Our Past

A Missouri resource we often forget is our state's history. Our historic sites and the special events with historic themes attract many visitors to the state. But it is also good for Missourians to visit these sites and take part in the special events. It reminds us about the hard work and bravery that made Missouri what it is today.

State Historic Sites

There are over 30 state historic sites. These are places where an important event took place or where someone famous once lived. Some demonstrate how life used to be in Missouri.

For example, at Deutschheim State Historic Site in Hermann, you can see how the early German settlers lived. The Battle of

Lexington State Historic Site is where an important Civil War battle took place. Harry S Truman's birthplace in Lamar is also a historic site.

Museums

Historic sites are one way to see Missouri's past. You also can visit history museums. Some are large, such as the Jefferson National Expansion Memorial Museum beneath the Gateway Arch in St. Louis. Others are small, like the two-room house in Rocheport.

Museums contain items used by people in the past and pictures and paintings of people and events from the past. Sometimes they contain displays that show how life used to be. Some museums tell about the history of a town or county, like the museum in Kennett. Some tell about a special event, like the Pony Express Museum in St. Joseph. Other museums tell about a person or group of persons, like the Bushwhacker Museum in Nevada.

The Museum of Westward Expansion, located below the Gateway Arch, contains artifacts, mounted animal specimens, an authentic American Indian tipi, and an overview of the Lewis and Clark expedition.

Many people across the state take part in re-enactments. They dress in appropriate clothes and assume roles, such as Civil War participants. This man is re-enacting the role of an early 19th-century Mississippi River trader.

Festivals and Re-enactments

Another way to remember Missouri's past is to attend a festival or re-enactment. Many Missouri communities hold festivals to celebrate their history and to remember the people who settled the community. For example, Monett celebrates Pioneer Days each September. Some people dress like pioneers. Others demonstrate how pioneers made tools. Still others play music and do some of the same dances the pioneers did. You can even taste food like the pioneer children used to eat.

Other festivals celebrate special events or people in a town's history. Sedalia was once home to Scott Joplin, a famous ragtime music composer. Each June, people come from all over the world to Sedalia to hear ragtime music. Clark County was once known for its mules, so every September there is the Mule Festival in Kahoka.

In some communities, re-enactments are put on by groups of people who have studied how Missourians used to live. You can watch them as they live just like people in the past. In Columbia, you can visit a Civil War camp and see the "soldiers" as they eat, practice marching, wash their clothes, and sometimes have a battle. In Boonville, you can see how crops were harvested and wheat threshed with steam-driven tractors.

Summary

In this chapter, you learned about Missouri's natural richness. You learned about its water, soil, minerals, wildlife, and forests and the importance of using these resources wisely. Wise use of our resources includes conservation and recycling and using alternative forms of energy that do not pollute the air or water. We can enjoy the state's natural beauty at its state parks and conservation areas.

You also learned how the state's history is a valuable resource. It not only attracts tourists to Missouri but also teaches us how hard people worked to make the state what it is today. We can learn about our history at state historic sites, museums, festivals, and re-enactments.

Chapter • Review

Reviewing Vocabulary

conservation
erosion
irrigate
minerals
natural resources
quarry
strip mining

On a sheet of paper, write the numbers 1 to 7. Beside each number, write the word or phrase from the list above that best completes the sentence.

1. Limestone is dug from a _____.
2. _____ takes place when water washes away or wind blows away the soil.
3. Open-pit mining is also called _____.
4. _____ involves using only the natural resources we need.
5. When it does not rain, farmers have to _____ their crops.
6. Soil, water, forests, and minerals are examples of _____ found in Missouri.
7. Plants use _____ from the soil as food to help them grow.

Reviewing Facts

1. Why is it important for farmers to rotate their crops?
2. Missouri produces most of the world's supply of what mineral?
3. In what ways is zinc used?
4. Where do we get our water in Missouri?
5. Name two alternative forms of energy.
6. Why are there hunting and fishing seasons?
7. Which state government agency manages our state forests?
8. Why do you think some communities hold festivals?

Using What You've Learned

1. Name two kinds of natural resources.
2. Why is some soil better than others for growing crops?
3. Name as many products that come from trees as you can think of.

Building Skills

1. What happens to the land after the coal is removed from a strip mine?
2. Why are trees important for the environment? Why are trees important for our economy? How can people use the trees for the economy without hurting our environment?

Did You Know?

- Crowder State Park near Trenton is named for Major General Enoch H. Crowder, the Missourian who founded the nation's Selective Service System, better known as the military draft.
- The granite columns on the front porch of the Governor's Mansion were quarried in Iron County.
- The study of trees is called dendrology.

Chapter Ten

Government in Missouri

T he state **Capitol**, the building in which the General Assembly meets, is located in Jefferson City. Carved above the door of the Capitol are the Latin words *Salus Populi Suprema Lex Esto*. These words are the state motto. In English, the motto means "Let the Welfare of the People Be the Supreme Law." The motto is meant to guide the state legislators, officials, and employees as they work. What kind of work do these people do? And what kind of work do county and city officials do?

State Government

Before Missouri could become a state, its territorial government had to write a constitution that explained how the new state would be governed. That constitution has been rewritten five times. The constitution we use today was written in 1945.

The constitution explains that Missouri's government has three branches: executive, legislative, and judicial. The three branches share power equally, but each has different duties.

Executive Branch

The **executive branch** is charged with making sure the state's laws are obeyed. The **governor** is the head of the executive branch and oversees the operation of the state. Other officials in the executive branch include the lieutenant governor, treasurer, auditor, secretary of state, and attorney general. Each of these people is elected to a four-year term. The governor is limited to two terms.

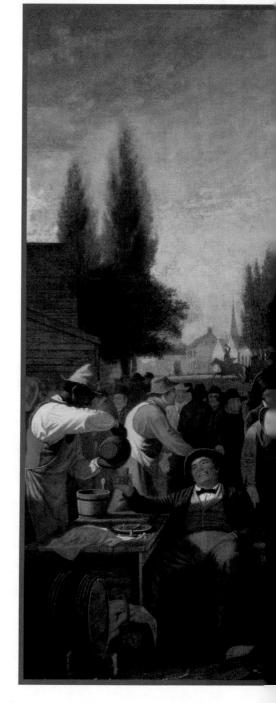

George Caleb Bingham painted the "County Election" to depict the activity surrounding local elections in the 1800s.

The governor appoints the directors and members of various commissions, the heads of some departments in the state government, and all state judges. The governor also signs the bills passed by the General Assembly, making them laws.

If the governor has to quit or dies while in office, the lieutenant governor would take his or her place. The lieutenant governor also presides over the state Senate, meaning he or she runs the sessions when the senators are working.

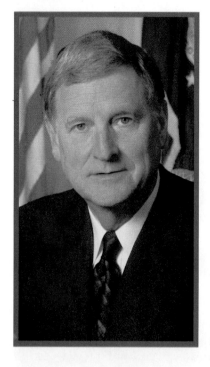

Above: Governor Mel Carnahan died October 16, 2000, in a plane crash. The governor had served two terms and was running for the U.S. Senate. He was killed on his way to a campaign event. Lieutenant Governor Roger B. Wilson became the new governor. Right: The Governor's Mansion in Jefferson City has been home to the state's governors since 1872.

Legislative Branch

The **legislative branch** is the group that makes laws for Missouri. Missouri's state legislature is called the **General Assembly**. It has two houses: the **House of Representatives** and the **Senate**.

There are 162 representatives and 34 senators. Each represents a particular district in the state. Each House district has about the same number of people in it, and each Senate district has about the same number of people. Representatives are elected to 2-year terms and senators to 4-year terms. But the members of the General Assembly can serve no more than 12 years.

The General Assembly is *in session* (meets) from January to May each year. Sometimes it meets in *special session* in times of an emergency. The governor called a special session after the Great Flood of 1993.

This chamber is where the Missouri House of Representatives meets.

Making Laws

A **bill** is a suggested law. A bill can be introduced in either the House of Representatives or the Senate. Let us follow a bill that is introduced in the House of Representatives. (The procedure is the same for the Senate.)

One part of a legislator's job is to listen to his or her **constituents**, the people who live in his or her district. Constituents let their representative know what laws might be needed or changed and how they believe the state's money should be spent. The representative uses this information when writing a bill.

The Great Flood of 1993 led the governor to call a special session of the General Assembly.

After writing the bill, the representative introduces it, or brings it before the rest of the House. The bill is sent to a **committee**, a group of representatives who study the bill. The committee might even decide to hold public meetings to find out how people feel about it. The committee then sends the bill back to the House for a vote, sometimes with amendments (additions or changes).

The rest of the House then votes on the bill. Other representatives can make amendments. If the bill passes, it is sent to the Senate. (Bills that pass in the Senate first are then sent to the House.) There the bill follows the same procedures.

The Senate might make amendments of its own or might write its own bill on the same subject. Often a bill passed by the Senate is different from the one passed by the House. Then the two bills are sent to a committee made up of both representatives and senators. This committee works out the differences. The compromise version of the bill is sent to both houses for a vote. If both houses approve the bill, it is sent to the governor to be signed into law.

If the governor does not like a bill, he or she can **veto** it, or refuse to approve it. The General Assembly can try to override (or pass) a bill that has been vetoed. But it takes the votes of two-thirds of the senators and two-thirds of the representatives to override the governor's veto.

Judicial Branch

The **judicial branch** is made up of the courts and judges of the state. In Missouri, there are three levels of courts: the supreme court, the court of appeals, and the circuit courts.

When someone breaks the law or files a lawsuit, the case is heard by the circuit court. If one of the people involved does not like the decision of the circuit court, he or she can appeal it to the court of appeals. To **appeal** means to ask that a higher-level court take another look at the case. The highest court in the state is the supreme court. The supreme court hears appeals from the lower courts.

All judges are appointed by the governor and, one year later, voted on by the voters. Judges on the supreme court and the court of appeals serve 12-year terms. Circuit court judges serve 6-year terms, and associate circuit court judges serve 4-year terms.

The Supreme Court meets in this building in Jefferson City. The judges hear cases each month from September through May.

The State Capitol

The Capitol in Jefferson City is actually the fourth building to house Missouri's state government. The first Capitol was in St. Charles, where the General Assembly and state officials shared the upstairs of a general store. The first Capitol in Jefferson City was completed in 1826. It burned down in 1837. It was replaced three years later by a new Capitol.

On the night of February 5, 1911, lightning struck the Capitol dome, setting it on fire. The fire spread quickly through the wooden roof and attic. Local residents, state officials, and even prisoners released from the nearby penitentiary rushed into the burning building and saved many of the state documents and artifacts.

Work on the new building began in 1913. It was 10 times larger than the previous Capitol and was finished in 1917. The walls of the 5-story building are made from Missouri limestone. Inside and out, there are 134 limestone columns. It took more than 750 railroad cars to carry the stone from the quarries! On the top of the dome is a statue of Ceres, the Roman goddess of agriculture. The dome is lighted at night and can be seen for miles.

Top: This statue of Thomas Jefferson in front of the Capitol honors the person responsible for the Louisiana Purchase. Above: One of the murals in the Capitol is this one by Missouri artist Thomas Hart Benton.

It took 11 years to finish decorating the inside. There are murals and paintings, beautiful mahogany doors, tall stained-glass windows, and statues. Carvings of proverbs, dogwood trees, acorns, and bears are everywhere. Each door handle has a copy of the state seal on it. And the water fountains feature bears that spout hot water from their mouths at the push of a button!

The Capitol is open every day except Christmas. You could take a guided tour. But it is just as much fun to roam through

the building. You can count dogwood flower carvings or bears, look at Civil War flags and a real stagecoach, or view murals that show the state's different regions and historic events.

The main function of the Capitol is to provide a work place for state government. The House of Representatives and the Senate each have a large room, or chamber, where they meet. Each representative and senator has an office as do the governor and other members of the executive branch.

Above left: A statue of Ceres tops the Capitol dome. *Top:* This statue in front of the Capital commemorates Missouri's statehood. *Above:* This stagecoach is just one exhibit in the State Museum of History in the Capitol.

*Above: The Buchanan County Courthouse in St. Joseph was built in the late 1800s. It is listed on the National Register of Historic Places. **Opposite** page: County government offices for Saline County are in this courthouse in Marshall.*

Local Governments

Missouri is divided into 114 counties, each with its own government. Within each county there are villages, towns, cities, school districts, and other special districts—and each of those has its own government.

County Government

Missouri's counties are divided into four "classes," depending on how much money they collect in property taxes. A county's class determines the type of government the county has. Boone, Buchanan, Clay, Franklin, Greene, Jackson, Jefferson, St. Charles, and St. Louis are all first-class counties. First-class counties generally have a **council** form of government. Under this type of government, the county is divided into districts, and a council member is elected from each district. The council and a county executive, who is also elected by the voters, make all the decisions for the county.

Most Missouri counties are second, third, or fourth class. These counties are governed by a **commission**. The commission is made up of two commissioners elected from districts and one commissioner who represents the whole county. The commission decides how to spend the county's money, but it does not pass laws. Laws for second-, third-, and fourth-class counties are passed by the General Assembly.

County officials, such as the county clerk, the sheriff, and the prosecuting attorney, may be elected or appointed.

City Government

Municipalities (villages, towns, or cities) in Missouri are divided into classes, depending on their population. A municipality with fewer than 500 people is called a **village**. Cities with fewer than 3,000 people are fourth-class municipalities. Those with fewer than 30,000 people are third class. Cities with more than 30,000 people used to be called second-class and first-class cities. Now they are called *charter* or *home-rule cities*.

The classes determine what type of government a municipality can have. For example, a village is only allowed to have a board of trustees. All other cities have some combination of mayor, city council, city manager, or city commis-

Springfield City Hall celebrated its 100th birthday in 1994. The building was a U.S. Customs House and Post Office. It is a National Register Historic Site.

sion. A city's classification also determines what types of laws the city government can pass.

Other Local Governments

There are other types of local governments in Missouri. Your local public school is part of a school district governed by an elected school board. The school board decides how the district's money will be spent. It also hires the teachers, cooks, and janitors and makes some of the rules.

Your county might also have a library district, a fire protection district, a water and sewer district, a levee district, an ambulance district, and a soil conservation district. Each district is governed by a board elected by the people living in the district.

Making It Work

Running a state, county, city, or school district takes people and money. Some of the people are elected. Others are hired by those who are elected. To be elected—or to vote in an election—a state citizen must be at least 18 years old and a registered voter. For some offices, a person must be older than 18 to be elected. For example, a person must be at least 35 to be elected governor.

The money needed to run state and local governments comes from various sources. Governments get most of their money from taxes. Taxes, you will remember, are the money people and businesses pay to the government. The government uses the taxes to pay for the services it provides. In Missouri, when you buy most items, you pay a state *sales tax*. People who

School districts are governed by an elected school board. The board makes many decisions, including those affecting transportation for school children.

Some of the money that the state of Missouri collects in taxes goes to pay for the up-keep and renovation of state buildings, such as the Capitol.

work in Missouri pay a state *income tax*. The state also collects fees, such as the fee to camp in a state park, the fee to get a copy of a birth certificate, or the fee for a driver's license.

Counties and cities also collect fees, sales taxes, and property taxes. A *property tax* is a tax on property owned, such as a house, land, a business, or a car. School districts and other districts get a part of the property taxes collected by the county.

Missourians also pay federal taxes. Some of that money is given back to the state and local governments. Some of it comes back to the state when the federal government buys products made in Missouri, such as military planes.

Not many people like to pay taxes. But the money collected in taxes and fees helps pay for all kinds of services. Some of these services are new roads, street lights, school books and teachers' salaries, testing for clean water, fire and police protection, state parks, food for poor people, help when there is a disaster, advertising to attract tourists, and much more.

Summary

In this chapter you learned about state and local government. The type of government we have is set out in the state constitution. You learned that there are three branches of state government: executive, legislative, and judicial. You also learned how a bill becomes law.

You learned that Missouri's 114 counties are divided into classes based on the amount collected in property taxes. Its municipalities are also divided into classes, based on population. These classifications determine the type of government a county or municipality can have.

Chapter • Review

Reviewing Vocabulary

bill
Capitol
constituents
General Assembly
municipality
veto
village

On a sheet of paper, write the numbers 1 to 7. Beside each number, write the word or phrase from the list above that best completes each of the following sentences.

1. The _____ is the building where the state legislature meets.
2. _____ is another name for a village, town, or city.
3. _____ are the people represented by a legislator.
4. Missouri's legislature is called the _____.
5. A _____ has fewer than 500 residents.
6. A proposed law, called a _____, can be introduced in either house of the legislature.
7. If the governor dislikes a bill passed by the legislature, she or he can try to keep it from becoming law with a _____.

Reviewing Facts

1. What are the three branches of the state government?
2. Who would take the governor's place if the governor dies or quits before his or her term is over?
3. What are the two houses of the General Assembly?
4. Describe the steps a bill takes on its way to becoming law.
5. How can the legislature override a governor's veto?
6. What are the three levels of courts in our state?
7. What can a person do if he or she does not agree with the decision of a court?
8. Where do governments get most of their money?

Using What You've Learned

1. What classification is your county? What type of government does it have?
2. Name two services that your local government provides.

Building Skills

1. Prepare a chart of all the elected officials who represent you at either the state or the local level of government.
2. Pretend you are a state legislator. What is one bill you would introduce and why?

Did You Know?

- The 12th president of the United States was David Rice Atchinson, a Missouri senator who served for one day in 1849.
- The Ford brothers were tried for the murder of Jesse James in the Buchanan County Courthouse in St. Joseph.

Government in Missouri

Chapter Eleven

Show Me Missouri

Want to go for a ride? Then you had better hurry, because our tour of Missouri begins in State Line. Quick! Look on the map! Where is State Line? There it is, way down in Pemiscot County in the Bootheel of southeast Missouri.

The Southeast Lowlands

On Highway 61 in State Line, we are standing on the imaginary line between Missouri and Arkansas. Above us is an arch over the highway. To visitors coming from Arkansas it says, "Entering Missouri."

As we ride north through Braggadocio, you will notice how flat the land around here is. On one side of the road, there are long rows of cotton plants with their white blossoms. On the other side of the road is what looks like grass sticking up in a field covered with water. That is a rice paddy, a field where rice is grown.

Heading north and west, we drive by orchards full of peach trees. Off in the distance, past Campbell, is what looks like a line of hills. That's Crowley's Ridge, which stretches from Arkansas across southeast Missouri toward the northeast.

The Bootheel swamplands are now some of the world's best farms. This Pemiscot County farm grows cotton.

215

ouri: *The Show Me State*

When the great New Madrid earthquakes of 1811 and 1812 struck the Bootheel, the earth split open. Sand poured from the crack, piling up into this long, high ridge.

Trail of Tears

Driving east and north, we go through New Madrid (the town that gave the earthquakes their name) and then Sikeston. A little farther north, we stop at Bollinger Mill and walk across Missouri's oldest covered bridge. It was built in 1867. Then we turn eastward to reach Cape Girardeau, a former riverboat town named for an early French trader. It is home to Southeast Missouri State University.

We follow the Mississippi River upstream to Trail of Tears State Park. In 1838, the United States government forced much of the Cherokee Indian Nation out of North Carolina. The Cherokee had to walk to their new reservation in Oklahoma. It was here that they crossed the Mississippi into Missouri—

in the middle of winter. Their journey became known as the "Trail of Tears" because of the terrible conditions they went through. Cold weather, a long and dangerous route, and a lack of food left the Cherokee weak and sick. One-fourth of them died along the way. According to legend, one of those who died was Princess Otahki, the daughter of a chief. A memorial to her is in the park.

Ste. Genevieve

Did you notice that the land became much more hilly as we went north from the Bootheel? That is because we are on the eastern edges of the Ozark Mountains.

Around the town of Mine LaMotte, we will meet people who still speak French to each other. In 1732, some of their ancestors grew tired of crossing the Mississippi River from Fort Kaskaskia to reach their mines and farms. They started a village on the Missouri side of the river that came to be known as Ste. Genevieve. In Ste. Genevieve, there are a number of houses that are more than 200 years old.

Above: The 1785 home of Jean Baptiste Valle in Ste. Genevieve. Valle was the last Spanish commandant and the first American governor of Ste. Genevieve Territory. Opposite page, top: This covered bridge in Burfordville is the oldest in the state. It was completed just after the Civil War. Opposite page, below: The Court of Common Pleas in Cape Girardeau hears local civil disputes.

Going north, we come to Washington State Park near De Soto. Here we can see **petroglyphs**, rock carvings left by the prehistoric Indians. The Indians held ceremonies in the woods along the Big River.

St. Louis

Just a short distance north along Interstate 55 is St. Louis. There is much to see and do in the St. Louis area. We can ride to the top of the Gateway Arch and visit the Zoo and the Science Center. We can tour the Art Museum and the National Museum of Transportation. At the Jefferson Memorial in Forest Park, we can visit a museum to learn more about Missouri history.

We cross the Missouri River from St. Louis County to St. Charles. There, we can stand on the riverfront and imagine we are watching Lewis and Clark begin their "Voyage of Discovery." We can also visit the first state Capitol and take a bike ride on the Katy Trail.

Heading west along the river, we come to Defiance. Here we can take a tour of Daniel Boone's home. We can even sit beneath the giant oak tree where Daniel sometimes sat as a Spanish judge, listening to court cases. Along here, the Missouri River runs through a valley with high bluffs on each side. Some of the early German settlers wrote to their friends that this part of Missouri was "just like home." This also is the beginning of Missouri's grape-growing and wine-making region.

The Lead Belt

As we go south, we enter another mining region of Missouri. Town names such as Valles Mines, Hematite, Old Mines, Mineral Point, Leadington, Graniteville, and Ironton remind us of the area's mining heritage. There is still a large iron ore mine near Fletcher.

Near Bonne Terre, which is French for "good earth," the St. Joe Lead Company had a huge underground mine. After all

*Opposite page, top: The Gateway Arch in St. Louis soars 630 feet above the Mississippi River. **Opposite page, below:** The Old Courthouse in St. Louis was the scene of the original case involving slave Dred Scott. **Below:** The St. Joseph Lead Co. operated this mine in Park Hills from 1906 until 1972. Today it is a state historic site.*

the lead ore was removed, the mine closed. Springs filled the mine with water. Today, people scuba dive into the mine and explore its various passageways to see the mining equipment left behind.

At Park Hills, we can visit the Missouri Mines State Historic Site. There we can tour mine buildings, see old mining equipment, and learn about mining in Missouri.

Scenic Waterways

Down the highway, we come to a high, round mountain called Pilot Knob. At the foot of the hill is Fort Davidson, where there was an important Civil War battle. We will take a side trip to Johnson Shut-Ins State Park near Lesterville, where the Black River rushes through a maze of rocks. A nice hike up the Ozark Trail takes us past Mina Sauk Falls and brings us to the top of Taum Sauk Mountain, Missouri's highest point.

The Black River begins in the Ozark Mountains. It flows through Johnson's Shut-ins State Park before making its way to Arkansas.

We are not too far from Elephant Rocks State Park. There, huge pink granite rocks the size of elephants stand in a line as if put there by a giant circus trainer!

Now we head west and south, up and down hilly roads that cut through forests that seem to stretch to the horizon. In Carter County, we come to Big Spring, where millions of gallons of water pour out from the ground every day. The spring's crystal-clear, cold waters run into the Current River, a part of the Ozark National Scenic Riverways. Many people like to canoe and fish on the Current, Jacks Fork, and Eleven Point rivers and on other Ozark streams.

As we turn back north, we go through parts of the Mark Twain National Forest and the town of Viburnum. This is the world's largest lead-mining district. Deep in the ground below us, miners are working to dig out the lead ore.

German Settlements

Now we leave the Ozarks behind for a while, but not the hilly land. As we head north into Maries and Osage counties, you will see long, low buildings with screened windows on the sides. These are turkey barns. In one of these barns, your Thanksgiving turkey might be growing!

Town names like Westphalia, Freeburg, and Frankenstein tell us this was an area settled by German immigrants. Hermann is another one of those towns. Each spring and fall, Hermann has huge festivals with lots of German food and music.

Hermann has over 100 buildings and two districts listed on the National Register of Historic Places. This is the Maria Waechter House, built in 1863.

The Glacial Plains

Crossing the Missouri River at Hermann, we head north and east through Montgomery City, Vandalia, and Bowling Green. At Clarksville, on the Mississippi River, we climb the highest bluff on the river. Below us we can see the river and the lock and dam. In the winter, hundreds of bald eagles fly down from Alaska. They spend the winter here, feeding on fish they find in the ice-free water below the dam.

This is Mark Twain's boyhood home in Hannibal. Who do you suppose whitewashed the fence to the right?

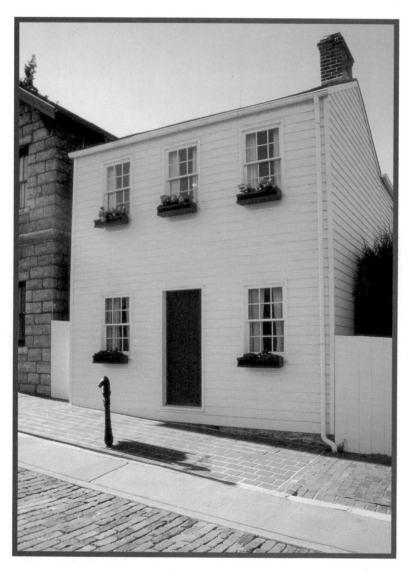

Mark Twain Country

North through Louisiana, past fruit tree nurseries and dairy farms with miles of white fences, we come to Hannibal. This is the boyhood home of Samuel Clemens. We know him better as Mark Twain. Here we can visit the house where young Sam grew up. We can tour the cave where Tom Sawyer and Becky Thatcher ran into Injun Joe. During Tom Sawyer Days in July, we can even take a turn whitewashing a fence!

From Hannibal, we go north to St. Patrick. Many Irish immigrants settled in this area of northern Missouri. Some of them came to help build the railroads. They stayed behind to start towns like St. Patrick. Thousands of letters pass through the town's tiny post office each St. Patrick's Day to get the town's special postmark.

We head south from St. Patrick. The land here is made up of gently rolling hills, some of them covered with sheep. Around Labor Day (the first Monday in September), the World Sheep Fest is held in Bethel. There are hundreds of sheep on display, as well as sheep dog contests, booths selling wool, food, crafts, and music.

As we travel south, we come to a sign for Paris. Then we see a sign pointing one way to Florida and the other way to Mexico. Where are we? Well, we are still in Missouri, but these towns have taken their names from other famous places. Florida is a small village on Mark Twain Lake. That is a good name for the lake, because Florida is where Samuel Clemens was born.

The State Capital

As we drive through Mexico, you will notice there are a lot of horses on the farms. The land is much flatter. The fields are filled with corn and soybeans.

Farther south is Fulton and a church called St. Mary Aldermanbury, which is more than 800 years old. The church was brought from London—stone by stone, board by board. It was a gift from the British people in honor of a 1946 visit by Winston Churchill. Churchill, the former prime minister of Great Britain, gave a speech at Westminster College in Fulton. In that speech, he referred to the "iron curtain" that divided the Soviet Union and its allies from the rest of the world. Next to the

A statue of Winston Churchill stands in front of St. Mary Aldermanbury Church in Fulton. When the Berlin Wall fell, Churchill's granddaughter got a section of it to create a sculpture, entitled "Break Through," to commemorate her grandfather's Iron Curtain speech at Fulton.

church and museum is a piece of the Berlin Wall, a part of that "iron curtain."

Continuing south, we reach the Missouri River Valley again. As we come down the hill, you can see the dome of the Capitol standing tall over the river. This is Jefferson City, our capital. Between January and May, the General Assembly is at work in the Capitol. Perhaps we will get to see our legislators at work. Besides visiting the Capitol, we can tour a museum on state history and state resources. The Capitol also has many famous paintings, including a mural by Thomas Hart Benton. A **mural** is a large painting on a wall.

From Jefferson City, we go back north to Columbia, home to the University of Missouri and the State Historical Society of Missouri. Just outside of town is Rock Bridge Memorial State Park. A boardwalk trail takes us under and over a rock bridge and past a cave called the Devil's Ice Box.

This page: At the Jefferson Landing State Historic Site in Jefferson City, you can see the 1839 Lohman Building (right), a three-story limestone structure used as a grocery, general store, warehouse, and hotel. The 1855 Missouri Hotel (above) was renamed the Union Hotel after the Civil War. Opposite page, top: The Old Saline County Courthouse in Arrow Rock was supposedly the scene of the painting on pages 202-203. Opposite page, below: Along Rocheport's Main Street, you will see the old Bank of Rocheport, now the post office.

Trailheads

West of Columbia is Rocheport, a former steamboat town. Several old buildings from the steamboat days are still standing. This is a good place to walk on the Katy Trail, following the river in one direction or going through a tunnel in the other direction.

West of Rocheport is Franklin, where the Santa Fe Trail once started. We cross over the river into Boonville and then follow the river upstream. In some of the fields, you can see ruts left long ago by the wagons starting out on the Santa Fe Trail. Upriver, we come to Arrow Rock, another starting place for the trail. Arrow Rock has preserved, or saved, many of the old buildings that were here when the settlers set out on their trip west.

Crossing back over the river at Glasgow, we go north past fields of plants with large golden leaves. These are tobacco plants. This is one of two regions in Missouri where tobacco is grown.

The Green Hills

After Salisbury, we go east to Moberly, then north through Macon. Soon we reach Kirksville, home to Truman State University. This part of Missouri was settled by families who moved here from Kentucky, Tennessee, and Virginia. They loved how green the trees and prairie grasses seemed. You can tell, because there is a Green City, a Greencastle, a Greensburg, and a Green Top. All of them are within a short drive of Kirksville. The rolling hills around here are even called the Green Hills.

Northern Missouri is one of the state's coal-mining regions. The town of Novinger, just west of Kirksville, holds a festival each year celebrating its coal-mining heritage. From Novinger, we turn south, passing by Elmer and Ethel on our way to Marceline, where Walt Disney spent part of his childhood. The highway south takes us to Brunswick and the mouth of the Grand River, where Fort Orleans once stood. The groves (groups of trees) on either side of the road are pecan trees. Most of the pecans grown in Missouri come from this region.

Kirksville is home to Truman State University. This is a photograph of Pickler Memorial Library.

We follow the Grand River upstream to Swan Lake National Wildlife Refuge. In the fall, millions of birds migrating (flying) south stop here to rest and eat. In the spring, they stop again on their way back north.

West of here is Hamilton, the hometown of James Cash Penney. He started the chain of department stores that bears his name—JC Penney. We will stop at the covered bridge at Locust Creek on the way.

Not far from Hamilton is Jamesport. There are several areas in the state that are home to people whose religious beliefs lead them to shun (keep away from) cars and other modern inventions. Some of these people are called Mennonites. Others, including those who live near Jamesport, are called Amish.

The Amish travel in horse-drawn buggies and wagons. They use draft horses to pull their plows. The people dress in plain, dark-colored clothes with no buttons or jewelry. Men and boys wear straw hats and suspenders. The women and girls wear bonnets. Most of the men have beards.

The large barns on Amish farms are decorated with designs that are supposed to keep away bad luck. Many of the farms sell fresh vegetables, homemade breads and candy, furniture, and quilts and other hand-sewn items to visitors. Some of the Amish operate stores and blacksmith and buggy-making shops.

We return south through Chillicothe and cross the Missouri River at Miami. We follow Highway 41 to Marshall. The land around here is very flat. The soil is very rich. This is where much of the corn is grown in Missouri. Farther south, we pass through Sedalia, where the State Fair is held for 10 days each August.

The Amish in the Jamesport area use a horse and carriage to get around.

The Ozark Highlands

Now we head east through Tipton and south to reach the Lake of the Ozarks. The lake is one of the most popular tourist attractions in Missouri. People come here from all over the Midwest to fish, swim, and go boating. The lake has 1,300 miles of shoreline. That is more than Lake Michigan and more than the Pacific coast of California. We can also visit the dam that created the lake and see the generating plant. Here water coming through gates in the dam turns turbines to generate electricity.

In 1905, Robert Snyder, a businessman from Kansas City, chose a site in what is now Ha Ha Tonka State Park to build a European-style mansion, often referred to as the castle. In 1942, a fire gutted the castle. Today, only the masonry walls remain.

Going south through Lebanon, we come to Mansfield, where Laura Ingalls Wilder and her family lived after moving to Missouri. Here she wrote books about growing up on the frontier, including *Little House on the Prairie*.

In Mansfield, we are back in the Ozarks. If we go east, we can find towns with names like Mountain Grove and Mountain View. The hills are covered with hawthorn bushes and hickory and oak trees. There is an occasional small clearing with a few cows. Small cabins cling to the steep hillsides.

Branson

In contrast to the usually quiet Ozark hills is the town of Branson, south and west of Mansfield. Millions of people come here every year to hear their favorite country music stars. Almost lost in the glitter and glare of lights is Silver Dollar City, a tourist attraction filled with displays of how life used to be in the hillbilly days. There you can see blacksmiths, coopers, spinning wheels, and other hand-crafted items.

Hillbillies

Settlers in the Ozarks of southern Missouri and northern Arkansas were once called *hillbillies*. Visitors believed the hillbillies were poor because they didn't have cars or electricity or other nice things. But the hillbillies could not afford to buy much because they raised just enough food to feed their families. They had little left over to sell or trade.

Others thought hillbillies were lazy because they were so poor. But living in the hills was hard. To clear enough land for crops to feed themselves and their animals meant years of hauling heavy rocks and tree stumps from the fields. Water had to be hauled in buckets from the streams. Almost everything had to be made by hand.

Hillbilly life could be fun, too. Without money to buy things, the hillbillies' lives were a lot less worrisome. They depended a lot on their religious faith and on preachers who traveled from church to church on mules. Family gatherings were times of celebration, filled with fiddle music and clog dancing.

The steep hills and rushing streams made traveling hard, so few people ever visited or left. For many hill people, their only education was learning to read the Bible. The language they spoke was a lot like the old-fashioned English they read in their Bibles.

New roads, electricity, and other modern conveniences have brought an end to the hillbilly way of live. But you can still find a cabin or two back in the woods where the people are happy to do without "all those new-fangled contraptions."

Settlers in the Ozark Mountains were often isolated. There were few roads, and transportation was often a wagon. Those who lived in the mountains had to make do with what they had or do without. This man is making baskets in which to gather and store things.

The Western Plains

North of Branson are Springfield and Wilson's Creek National Battlefield, the site of a famous Civil War battle. Springfield is Missouri's third-largest city and home to several colleges, including Southwest Missouri State University.

West on Interstate 44, past cattle ranches and dairy farms, is Joplin. Joplin was a **boom town**, a town that grew up almost

Above: Southwest Missouri State University in Springfield was founded in 1905. ***Right:*** Springfield is Missouri's third-largest city. The downtown area has a number of historic houses and buildings.

overnight when coal and other valuable minerals were found nearby. This is still an important mining region.

North of Carthage is Lamar, the birthplace of Harry S Truman. Here we can stop and tour the house where he was born. Still farther north, near Walker, the last patches of prairie can be found along the Osage River. The Osage Indians had several villages here. Standing in the tall grass, you might imagine you are an Osage looking out across the prairie at herds of bison.

Lexington

Now we head east and north toward Clinton. Along the way, we pass chicken hatcheries and cross Truman Reservoir, which was formed by another dam on the Osage River. Highway 13 takes us through Warrensburg (the home of Central Missouri State University) and Higginsville. We pass the Confederate Memorial State Historic Site. Then we reach the former steamboat port of Lexington. Here, we can visit a Civil War battlefield and see the cannonball that is still stuck in a column of the courthouse. Before crossing the Missouri River, we pause

Harry S Truman's birthplace in Lamar is now a state historic site.

at the Madonna of the Trail, a statue of a pioneer woman looking out over the valley below.

Independence

Heading north and west on Highway 10, we reach Excelsior Springs, where we visit the Hall of Waters. The hall was built during the Great Depression as a way to put people to work. You can learn about the many springs in the area and can even sample some of the mineral spring waters.

Going south through Liberty, we stop briefly at Fort Osage near Sibley. This was an important trading post after the Missouri Territory became part of the United States. The fort has been rebuilt as it was in 1820. We can see how people lived in and around the fort.

Then we come to Independence, famous as a starting place for the trails to the West. A visitors' center tells about pioneer trails, wagon trains, and steamboats. Independence was also

Fort Osage near Sibley was built in 1808. It was a government trade center and controlled all of the traffic up and down the Missouri River. When the government abandoned the fort, settlers took the lumber until nothing was left but the foundation stones. The fort was reconstructed beginning in 1948.

the home of Harry Truman. We can visit his library and home. At another museum, we learn about the Mormons, another religious group that settled in Missouri.

South of Independence are Blue Springs and Missouri Town. Here you can see a re-creation of a typical Missouri town that shows what life on the frontier was like 150 years ago.

A dogtrot tavern (above left) and a general store (above right) are two of the buildings you can see at Missouri Town to see what life was like in our state around 1855.

Kansas City

Approaching Kansas City from the east, the tall buildings on the horizon look like the Emerald City in *The Wizard of Oz*. There is no wizard to visit in Kansas City, but there are plenty of things to see.

We can stand near the Liberty Memorial and see the big bend in the Missouri River where it is joined by the Kansas River. We can see what is left of the famous stockyards. The nearby American Royal is an arena where a big rodeo and a horse and cattle show are held each November. At the Negro League Baseball Museum, we can learn all about teams like the Monarchs and Grays and about players like Satchel Paige and Cool Papa Bell. Other places to see are the Swope Park Zoo and the Nelson Art Gallery.

Many people visit Kansas City to see Country Club Plaza and its Spanish-style buildings. This was the first shopping center ever built in the United States. Each year at Christmas time, the buildings are lined with lights.

Kansas City is known by some people as the "Fountain City" because it has so many fountains. The only city in the world with more fountains is Rome, Italy!

St. Joseph

If we follow the Missouri River north out of Kansas City, we come to Weston. The hills around here are covered with fields of tobacco and tall, narrow tobacco barns where the leaves are hung to dry.

Still farther north on the river is St. Joseph, an important pioneer town. This is where the Pony Express began. You can still see the stables where the riders picked up the mail and jumped on their ponies before crossing the river on a ferry.

Northeast of St. Joseph, through the towns of Union Star and King City, the land is almost flat. As we near Conception, we see a huge church on the horizon. That is Conception Abbey, where monks spend their days printing books and cards.

We follow the highway across the Hundred and Two River to Maryville, home of Northwest Missouri State University. Then we push west through Tarkio and on to Rock Port. Here our tour ends—looking across the Missouri River to Nebraska.

There is much we did not see on our tour of Missouri. Perhaps on our way home, we will take a different route and see some more of the Show Me State!

Opposite page, top: Kansas City was once described as "one of the loveliest cities on Earth." Opposite page, below: One of Kansas City's many fountains. Below: Conception Abbey was founded in 1873.

Chapter Twelve

Missouri's People

You have read about Missouri's history, its geography, its resources, and its economy. But perhaps the best thing about Missouri is its people. In this chapter, you will learn about some well-known people who were either born in Missouri or who made Missouri their home at one time and can be called Missourians.

Well-Known Missourians

Some people from Missouri have become well known for the things they have done. They probably began much like you.

Maya Angelou

When Bill Clinton became president in January 1993, Maya Angelou was asked to read her poem "On the Pulse of the Morning." Angelou was born in St. Louis in 1928. Growing up was hard for her because of the Great Depression, her parents' divorce, and abusive relatives—all of which she wrote about in her first book, *I Know Why the Caged Bird Sings.*

Angelou did not let her hard childhood hold her back though. She moved to San Francisco and became the first woman streetcar conductor in the city. But her real desire was to be an actor, writer, and poet.

She has become famous for the many books and poems she has written about her life as an African-American woman. As an actor, she had a role in the television miniseries *Roots.* She has also acted on the Broadway stage, for which she won a Tony Award—the highest award a Broadway actor can receive.

Maya Angelou wrote a poem especially for Bill Clinton's inauguration. Here she is seen reading it on inauguration day.

Josephine Baker

Josephine Baker was born in St. Louis in 1901. When she was just a little girl, she danced and sang on the sidewalk outside a theater. The nickels and dimes people gave her went to buy food and "to keep warm" she said. It was not long before she was dancing and singing *inside* the theater.

Her talent took her to New York, where she was a star. She tried out for the famous Follies Bergere in France, where she became one of its biggest stars ever. Baker felt so comfortable in France that she became a French citizen in 1937. During World War II, Baker was a spy for the French against the Germans.

After the war, she worked to improve relations between the races. Baker and her husband adopted twelve children of different races. She often came back to the United States and St. Louis to speak out on civil rights. She stood with Dr. Martin Luther King, Jr., when he gave his "I Have a Dream" speech on the steps of the Lincoln Memorial in 1963. She died in 1975 and was given a hero's funeral in France.

Josephine Baker made her stage debut at the Booker T. Washington Theater, a black vaudeville house in St. Louis.

Count Basie

William Basie was born in Red Bank, New Jersey, in 1904. He learned to play the piano and became a jazz musician, picking up the nickname "Count."

In 1928, he came to Kansas City and joined Bennie Moten's Kansas City Orchestra, one of the leading jazz bands in the country. At the time, Kansas City attracted the country's best jazz musicians. The music they created was called the "Kansas City Sound." In 1936, Basie formed his own band, the Count Basie Orchestra. It quickly became one of the most popular bands in the country. The band sold thousands of records and appeared in several movies.

Count Basie (center) led one of the most important bands in jazz history. By the end of the 1930s, Count Basie's band was one of the most popular in the world.

Basie continued to perform after his band split up. He played on television specials and for presidents and the queen of England. In 1981, he was awarded a Kennedy Center Honor, one of the highest awards given a performer in this country. Count Basie died in 1984.

Above: Senator Thomas Hart Benton. ***Opposite page:*** Artist Thomas Hart Benton. ***Pages 244-245:*** The mural "Independence and the Opening of the West" by Thomas Hart Benton can be see at the Truman Library in Independence.

Thomas Hart Benton

There have been two famous Thomas Hart Bentons in Missouri history. The first Thomas Hart Benton was born in North Carolina and came to Missouri from Tennessee in 1814. He became an editor of the *Missouri Enquirer* and worked to make Missouri a state.

In 1820, when Missouri did become a state, Thomas Hart Benton was elected one of its first two U.S. senators. His work helped the frontier states by making it easier for small farmers and businessmen to buy land and start businesses. Benton was against slavery. That led to his defeat for re-election in 1851. He later served one term in the U.S. House of Representatives. Thomas Hart Benton, the politician, died in 1858.

The second Thomas Hart Benton was the grandnephew of the first one. He was born in Neosho in 1889 and began studying art as a teenager. Later he worked as a draftsman, a person who draws plans for buildings. He began painting scenes from Missouri and American history and folklore. He became famous for his murals, one of which appeared at the 1933 World's Fair in Chicago. He was asked to paint a mural of Missouri history for the lobby of the House of Representatives in the state Capitol. You can see that mural if you take a tour of the Capitol. You can also see Benton's work at the Truman Library in Independence and at the Country Music Hall of Fame in Nashville, Tennessee. Thomas Hart Benton, the artist, died in 1975.

Susan Blow

Susan Blow was born in St. Louis in 1843. A school teacher, she made a trip with her family to Germany. While there, she visited several private schools and saw a program the Germans called *kindergarten*, meaning "children's garden." The program was intended to help little children get used to going to school while teaching them simple things like shapes and colors and the alphabet.

In 1873, after her trip, she convinced William Harris, the superintendent of schools in St. Louis, to allow her to open the first public kindergarten in the United States. This was very important for the many immigrant children in St. Louis who did not speak English when they started school. Blow promised to work for free with two other volunteers. The school board hired a helper. They made the kindergarten a happy place, with flowers, lots of light and color, and music.

There were 38 children enrolled the first year. Before long, St. Louis had 30 kindergartens, more than any other American city. People came from all around the country to see the Missouri kindergartens. Soon the idea spread across the United States. Blow even started a school to help train kindergarten teachers.

*Above: This mural of Susan Blow is in the State Capitol in Jefferson City. **Opposite page, top:** Lucille Bluford finally received a degree from the University of Missouri—but it was an honorary degree. **Opposite page, below:** This painting of Daniel Boone was done by William C. Allen.*

Lucille Bluford

Lucille Bluford had graduated from the University of Kansas. She had become the managing editor of a newspaper—quite a feat for an African-American woman in 1939. But when she tried to enroll in the journalism school of the University of Missouri, she was told the university was not open to African Americans.

So Bluford sued the state to allow her into the journalism school. This was a brave act. The civil rights movement was not very strong and still very unpopular, especially in Missouri where schools were segregated. The court ruled that the university did not have to admit Bluford. But the state did have to provide a journalism school for black students at Lincoln University. Bluford enrolled at that school.

She went on to become a famous journalist. Later she was the editor of an African-American newspaper, the *Kansas City Call*. Under Bluford's editorship, the *Call* was a leader in the civil rights movement in Missouri. She was also one of the first persons appointed to the Missouri Human Rights Commission in 1957. In 1989, Bluford received an honorary doctorate degree—the school's highest honor—from the University of Missouri.

Daniel and Nathaniel Boone

Daniel Boone was a famous frontiersman who helped settle Kentucky. He and his sons often came to Missouri to hunt and trade furs with the Indians. Daniel's son, Nathaniel, moved to St. Charles County in 1798, near the present-day town of Defiance. Daniel visited often and later moved into a house near Nathaniel's.

At the time, Missouri was part of Spain's New World colonies. The Spanish governor made Daniel a judge. Daniel would often sit beneath a giant oak tree outside his house and hear court cases. You can still sit beneath that oak tree.

Nathaniel became famous as a leader of a militia unit that defended Missouri during the War of 1812. British soldiers and their Native American allies tried to take the Missouri Territory away from the United States. But Nathaniel and his soldiers drove them away.

Daniel Boone and his son built this house near Defiance with limestone from a nearby quarry. Daniel spent the remaining 17 years of his life here.

Daniel Boone died in his house in Defiance in 1820 at the age of 85. Nathaniel later moved to Springfield, where he died in 1856. You can visit both of their homes.

Daniel Boone was buried on a hilltop overlooking the Missouri River, next to his wife Rebecca. In 1845, the state of Kentucky asked that Daniel's and Rebecca's bodies be moved to Kentucky. But Daniel might still be buried in Missouri. Historians learned that Daniel had let a family friend use the gravesite everyone thought was his. No one is sure where Daniel's body was buried!

George Washington Carver

George Washington Carver was born a slave in 1864 near Diamond, in southwest Missouri. After his parents died, the people who owned him, Moses and Susan Carver, brought him up as their own son. When slavery was abolished, George remained on the Carver farm. There he learned to read and write.

George had to work at various jobs to pay for school and college. He enrolled in an Iowa college, intending to become an artist. But his real love was plants and how they grow. He transferred to Iowa State Agricultural College and earned a master's degree in agriculture.

In 1896, he became a teacher at Tuskegee Institute in Alabama, the famous school for blacks started by Booker T. Washington. Carver was interested in how crops were being grown in the South and how the soil was being destroyed. One problem was that farmers were growing cotton year after year in the same fields. This was robbing the soil of its nutrients.

Carver knew peanuts would grow in the soil of the South. By rotating peanuts with cotton, the nutrients in the soil could be replenished. But farmers couldn't make much money growing peanuts, so Carver began experimenting to find different uses for the peanut.

By the time he died in 1943, Carver had developed 300 products made from peanuts including face powder, printer's ink, soap, and a milk substitute. The most famous product, though, was peanut butter. Carver's work is credited with saving southern farmers.

You can visit the farm near Diamond to see where George Washington Carver was born and spent part of his boyhood. It is now a national historic site.

At Tuskegee Institute, George Washington Carver conducted research into uses for the peanuts grown by southern farmers.

Walt Disney

Walt Disney was born in Chicago in 1901 but grew up on a farm near Marceline. He started drawing at a young age and was selling his drawings to neighbors at age seven. It is said that he drew his first cartoon on the side of a neighbor's garage using a tar brush.

Disney later moved to Kansas City to go to art school. After graduating, he started drawing animated (moving) cartoons before going to Hollywood and opening his own studio. In 1928, he created his most famous character, Mickey Mouse. The Disney Studios went on to become famous for full-length animations such as *Snow White and the Seven Dwarfs* and *The Lion King*, movies like *Mary Poppins*, and weekly television shows. Disney won more than 100 prizes for his films, including 29 Academy Awards.

In 1955, Disney realized another dream with the opening of Disneyland, an amusement park in California. Walt Disney died in 1966. Today, there are also Disney parks in Florida, Japan, and France. The company started by Walt Disney owns a television network, hockey and baseball teams, and movie studios.

It was in Kansas City that Walt Disney became involved in animated cartoons. Later, he produced the first feature length animated film.

Rose Philippine Duchesne

In 1818, Rose Philippine Duchesne, a Roman Catholic nun, came to St. Charles from France with four other nuns. They planned to start a convent and a school for girls. At this time, there were no public schools in Missouri, and only rich families could afford to send their children to the few private schools. Mother Duchesne's school was different because it allowed poor girls to attend for free—the first free school west of the Mississippi.

Mother Duchesne later traveled all through the Missouri and Kansas territories. She started more than 40 schools—not only for white children but also for black children and Indian children. She even lived among the Indians in Kansas for a while. But her health forced her to return to the Sacred Heart Convent in St. Charles.

Mother Duchesne died in 1852. In 1988, the Roman Catholic Church said that Mother Duchesne had done so much good for others that she should be declared a saint. St. Rose Duchesne is only the fifth American and the first Missourian to be so honored.

Charles A. Lindbergh

In 1927, just flying across the state without stopping was a big deal. That is why it was hard to imagine someone flying solo (all alone) across the ocean to France. But 25-year-old Charles A. Lindbergh imagined it.

Mother Rose Philippine Duchesne was made a saint in the Roman Catholic Church in 1988.

Lindbergh was an airmail pilot who flew a regular route into and out of St. Louis. His many close calls flying the mail through bad weather had earned him the nickname "Lucky Lindy." He was always looking for faster and better airplanes and ways to make the public excited about flying.

Lindbergh set out to design a plane that could fly the long distance to France. A group of St. Louis businessmen helped pay for the new plane, which Lindbergh called the *Spirit of St. Louis.*

Lindbergh took off from an airfield on Long Island, New York, on May 20, 1927. To save weight for extra fuel, he had no radio and no parachute. Once he left sight of the shore, no one could know how he was doing or if he was even still alive.

It was hard to stay awake for so long. Once Lindbergh awoke to find his plane touching the ocean. He wasn't sure his com-

pass was working. He had to guess that he was going the right way. Just as night fell on the second day, he saw the lights of Paris ahead of him. He landed at 10 p.m., having flown 3,600 miles in 33 hours and 30 minutes. The large crowd carried him away on their shoulders.

When he returned to the United States, he was treated like a hero. Many cities held parades in his honor. The flight did as it was intended and got more people interested in flying. Before long, people were flying as passengers between cities.

Dred and Harriet Scott

Before the Civil War, there was a law that said a slave who was taken to live in a free state or territory had to be freed. He or she could not be brought back into a slave state and made a slave again. But that is just what happened to a man named Dred Scott and his wife Harriet. Their owner, John Emerson, had taken them as slaves into Illinois, a free state, and Minnesota, then a free territory. They should have been given their freedom. Instead, Emerson brought them back to Missouri as slaves. Dred Scott hired a lawyer and sued for their freedom.

The state supreme court ruled against the Scotts. The case was heard in the federal circuit court in St. Louis (which also ruled against them) and was appealed to the U.S. Supreme Court. In 1857, the Supreme Court ruled that the Scotts could not sue for their freedom because slaves were considered property and not citizens. As "property," they had no right to sue. In the end, however, the Scotts were bought by a friend who gave them their freedom.

Helen Stephens

Imagine being just 18 years old and the "fastest woman on earth." That is what people called Helen Stephens. She was born in Fulton in 1918 and grew up on a nearby farm. In high school, she was only 15 when she tied the world records for the 50-yard dash and the long jump. People started calling her the "Fulton Flash." In 1936, Stephens set a world record in the 100-meter dash and won gold medals in the 100-meter and 400-meter dashes at the Olympics. Her record in the 100-meter dash stood until 1960. After the Olympics, Stephens played professional basketball and put on track and field demonstrations.

She served in the Marine Corps in World War II. Then she went to work for the federal government until she retired. She did not let retirement slow her down, though. She competed in the Senior Olympics and became a spokesperson for the Show Me State Games. Helen Stephens died in 1994.

Opposite page, top: Charles Lindbergh and the Spirit of St. Louis, *in which he flew across the Atlantic.* **Opposite page, below:** *Dred Scott, a Missouri slave, sued unsuccessfully for his freedom.* **Below:** *Helen Stephens's world record in the 100 meters—11.5 seconds at the 1936 Olympics—stood for 24 years.*

Mark Twain (Samuel Clemens) was photographed visiting his boyhood home in Hannibal in 1902.

Mark Twain

Samuel Clemens was born in the small village of Florida. He grew up in nearby Hannibal, watching riverboats go up and down the Mississippi. He became a riverboat pilot and later a famous author, calling himself "Mark Twain." Those two words were used by river-boat crews when they threw a weighted line into the river to measure how deep the water was. If the river was deep enough for the boat, they would yell back to the pilot, "mark twain!"

Many of Mark Twain's books were about the adventures of growing up along the river. His books included a group of friends—Tom Sawyer, Huckleberry Finn, Becky Thatcher, and a runaway slave named Jim. Perhaps Mark Twain's most famous book is *The Adventures of Huckleberry Finn*, which told of Jim and Huck's trip down the Mississippi on a raft.

Twain also wrote about his adventures as a miner and a newspaper writer in the West and in Hawaii. His books are famous around the world. Mark Twain is considered one of our country's greatest writers.

Laura Ingalls Wilder

When Laura Ingalls was a little girl, her family moved from a cabin in the woods of Wisconsin to the prairies of Kansas. There she grew up, married Alonzo Wilder, and moved to South Dakota. **Drought** (a long period without rain) and hard times made Laura, Alonzo, and their daughter Rose move once again, this time to Missouri.

The Wilders arrived in Mansfield in 1894. After Alonzo died, Laura began writing stories about pioneer life for newspapers and magazines. Rose convinced her to write books about her adventures as a little girl. Laura's first book, *Little House in the Big Woods*, was published in 1932. It was very popular.

Laura then wrote *Little House on the Prairie*, about her family's adventures in Kansas and South Dakota. There were several Little House books, which were later made into a television series. Laura Wilder lived on her Rocky Ridge farm in Mansfield until her death in 1957.

Laura Ingalls Wilder's Little House *books have been a favorite of children and adults alike since they were first published in the 1930s.*

You have just read about 18 Missourians who have become well known or honored because they have done something important. Those 18 were selected because they came from all parts of the state, and they did different things. Some were scientists; some were educators; some were politicians; some were athletes; some were entertainers; and some were writers.

There are many more Missourians who have become well known. You may have heard of some of them, or your teacher

may want you to find out more about them. Here are more names of well-known Missourians.

- Yogi Berra, baseball player
- Chuck Berry, rock-and-roll singer and composer
- George Caleb Bingham, artist who painted scenes of the early frontier
- Bill Bradley, professional basketball player and later U.S. Senator from New Jersey
- William Wells Brown, a former slave who became an abolitionist
- Grace Bumbry, opera singer
- Dale Carnegie, writer and lecturer on how to make friends and have people listen to your ideas
- Kit Carson, frontiersman and explorer
- Kate O'Flaherty Chopin, author
- Walter Cronkite, radio and television newsperson
- Sheryl Crow, pop music singer
- Redd Foxx, comedian and actor
- Dick Gregory, comedian and civil rights activist
- Edwin Hubble, astronomer for whom the Hubble Telescope is named
- James Langston Hughes, author
- Herman Jaeger, farmer who developed a disease-resistant strain of grapes
- Annie Malone, businesswoman who started a line of hair care products
- Mary Margaret McBride, radio show host
- Mark McGwire, baseball player
- Marlin Perkins, wildlife conservationist, television show host, and former director of the St. Louis Zoo
- Vincent Price, actor
- Joseph Pulitzer, newspaper publisher for whom the Pulitzer Prize in journalism is named
- Casey Stengel, baseball player and manager
- Dick Van Dyke, television and movie actor
- Hiram Young, former slave who made many of the covered wagons used by pioneers traveling west

*Top: Christopher "Kit" Carson grew up in Boone's Lick. He is famous as a trapper, scout, Indian agent, soldier, and legend of the West. **Above:** Dick Gregory was born in St. Louis. He became known as an entertainer, author, and civil rights leader. He ran for president in 1968.*

What Makes a Person Important

You have just learned about some of Missouri's well-known people. But not all important people become well known. People give different reasons for what makes a person important. Some say it is having lots of money and things. Others say it is being in an important job. Still others say it is having a lot of people who know who you are.

A person can be important without having any of those things. Missouri's people are an important resource to the state. That is because all people are important when they try to make things around them better. Here are some things we can all do to be important.

- Treat other people as we want to be treated.
- Help other people.
- Be kind to other people.
- Be honest and truthful.
- Have respect for the environment. That means
  Don't litter.
  Pick up trash that you find even if someone else left it.
  Don't destroy plants and animals.
- Do what is right for your state and country.

Your parents and teachers have probably taught you other things that you can do to be an important person. You can think of things also.

What do you think some of the well-known people you have read about would tell you to do? Many of them have talked with schoolchildren. They tell these children things like "Stay in school," "Don't give up," and "Always believe in yourself."

Maybe the words of Harry Truman in his last speech as president are good advice. He told the American people that, when he became president upon the death of President Roosevelt, he knew there were other people more qualified than he to be president. But he accepted the job he had to do. "And," said Truman, "I have tried to give it everything that was in me."

*Top: James Langston Hughes was born in Joplin. He started writing poetry in the eighth grade. He also wrote novels, short stories, plays, musicals and operas, radio and television scripts, and magazine articles. **Above:** Born in St. Joseph, Walter Cronkite was called "the most trusted man in America" as a newscaster.*

Missouri State Symbols

Animal
Missouri mule

Rock
Mozarkite

Bird
Eastern bluebird

Song
"Missouri Waltz"

Flower
Hawthorn blossom

Tree
Flowering dogwood

Folk dance
Square dance

Tree nut
Eastern black walnut

Fossil
Crinoid (sea lily)

State capital
Jefferson City

Insect
Honeybee

Entered Union
August 10, 1821

Mineral
Galena (lead)

Origin of name
Algonquin Indian tribe
named after Missouri River,
meaning "muddy water"

Motto
"Salus populi Suprema lex esto"
("Let the welfare of the people
be the supreme law.")

Number of counties
114

Musical instrument
Fiddle

Geographic center
Miller, 20 miles southwest of Jefferson City

Nickname
The Show Me State

Highest point
Taum Sauk Mountain, 1,772 feet

Missouri Counties

County Name	County Seat	Square Miles
Adair	Kirksville	567
Andrew	Savannah	436
Atchinson	Rock Port	542
Audrain	Mexico	692
Barry	Cassville	773
Barton	Lamar	597
Bates	Butler	849
Benton	Warsaw	729
Bollinger	Marble Hill	621
Boone	Columbia	687
Buchanan	St. Joseph	409
Butler	Poplar Bluff	698
Caldwell	Kingston	431
Callaway	Fulton	842
Camden	Camdenton	641
Cape Girardeau	Jackson	577
Carroll	Carrollton	695
Carter	Van Buren	509
Cass	Harrisonville	702
Cedar	Stockton	471
Chariton	Keytesville	758
Christian	Ozark	564
Clark	Kahoka	507
Clay	Liberty	403
Clinton	Plattsburg	423
Cole	Jefferson City	392
Cooper	Boonville	566

County Name	County Seat	Square Miles
Crawford	Steelville	744
Dade	Greenville	491
Dallas	Buffalo	543
Daviess	Gallatin	568
DeKalb	Maysville	425
Dent	Salem	755
Douglas	Ava	814
Dunklin	Kennett	547
Franklin	Union	922
Gasconade	Hermann	521
Gentry	Albany	493
Greene	Springfield	678
Grundy	Trenton	437
Harrison	Bethany	725
Henry	Clinton	729
Hickory	Hermitage	379
Holt	Oregon	456
Howard	Fayette	464
Howell	West Plains	927
Iron	Ironton	552
Jackson	Independence	611
Jasper	Carthage	641
Jefferson	Hillsboro	661
Johnson	Warrensburg	834
Knox	Edina	507
Laclede	Lebanon	768
Lafayette	Lexington	632

County Name	County Seat	Square Miles
Lawrence	Mt. Vernon	614
Lewis	Monticello	508
Lincoln	Troy	627
Linn	Linneus	620
Livingston	Chillicothe	537
McDonald	Pineville	542
Macon	Macon	797
Madison	Fredericktown	497
Maries	Vienna	527
Mercer	Princeton	454
Miller	Tuscumbia	593
Mississippi	Charleston	410
Moniteau	California	417
Monroe	Paris	670
Montgomery	Montgomery City	540
Morgan	Versailles	594
New Madrid	New Madrid	679
Newton	Neosho	627
Nodaway	Maryville	875
Oregon	Alton	792
Osage	Linn	606
Ozark	Gainesville	731
Pemiscot	Caruthersville	517
Perry	Perryville	473
Pettis	Sedalia	686
Phelps	Rolla	674
Pike	Bowling Green	673
Platte	Platte City	421
Polk	Bolivar	636
Pulaski	Waynesville	550
Putnam	Unionville	520

County Name	County Seat	Square Miles
Ralls	New London	481
Randolph	Huntsville	473
Ray	Richmond	568
Reynolds	Centerville	808
Ripley	Doniphan	632
St. Charles	St. Charles	558
St. Clair	Osceola	698
St. Francois	Farmington	451
St. Louis	Clayton	505
Ste. Genevieve	Ste. Genevieve	504
Saline	Marshall	755
Schuyler	Lancaster	308
Scotland	Memphis	439
Scott	Benton	423
Shannon	Eminence	1,004
Shelby	Shelbyville	501
Stoddard	Bloomfield	815
Stone	Galena	451
Sullivan	Milan	651
Taney	Forsyth	608
Texas	Houston	1,180
Vernon	Nevada	837
Warren	Warrenton	429
Washington	Potosi	762
Wayne	Greenville	763
Webster	Marshfield	594
Worth	Grant City	266
Wright	Hartville	682
St. Louis City		61

Governors of Missouri

Territorial Governor	Term of Office
Amos Stoddard	1804
William Henry Harrison	1805
James Wilkinson	1805 - 1807
Joseph Browne (acting)	1807
Frederick Bates (acting)	1807
Meriwether Lewis	1807 - 1809
Frederick Bates (acting)	1809 - 1810
Benjamin Howard	1810 - 1813
William Clark	1813 - 1820

State Governor	Term of Office	Political Party
Alexander McNair	1820 - 1824	Democratic-Republican
Frederick Bates	1824 - 1825	Democratic-Republican
Abraham J. Williams	1825 - 1826	Democratic-Republican
John Miller	1826 - 1832	Democratic-Republican
Daniel Dunklin	1832 - 1836	Democratic
Lilburn W. Boggs	1836 - 1840	Democratic
Thomas Reynolds	1840 - 1844	Democratic
Meredith Miles Marmaduke	1844	Democratic
John Cummins Edwards	1844 - 1848	Democratic
Austin Augustus King	1848 - 1853	Democratic
Sterling Price	1853 - 1857	Democratic
Trusten Polk	1857	Democratic
Hancock Lee Jackson	1857	Democratic
Robert Marcellus Steward	1857 - 1861	Democratic
Claiborne Fox Jackson	1861	Democratic
Hamilton Rowan Gamble	1861 - 1864	Unionist Provisional Governor
Willard Preble Hall	1864 - 1865	Unionist Provisional Governor
Thomas Clement Fletcher	1865 - 1869	Radical

State Governor	Term of Office	Political Party
Joseph Washington McClurg	1869 - 1871	Radical
Benjamin Gratz Brown	1871 - 1873	Liberal
Silas Woodson	1873 - 1875	Democratic
Charles Henry Hardin	1875 - 1877	Democratic
John Smith Phelps	1877 - 1881	Democratic
Thomas Theodore Crittenden	1881 - 1885	Democratic
John Sappington Marmaduke	1885 - 1887	Democratic
Albert Pickett Morehouse	1887 - 1889	Democratic
David R. Francis	1889 - 1893	Democratic
William Joel Stone	1892 - 1897	Democratic
Lon V. Stephens	1897 - 1901	Democratic
Alexander M. Dockery	1901 - 1905	Democratic
Joseph W. Folk	1905 - 1909	Democratic
Herbert S. Hadley	1909 - 1913	Republican
Elliot W. Major	1913 - 1917	Democratic
Frederick D. Gardner	1917 - 1921	Democratic
Arthur M. Hyde	1921 - 1925	Republican
Sam A. Baker	1925 - 1929	Republican
Henry S. Caulfield	1929 - 1933	Republican
Guy B. Park	1933 - 1937	Democratic
Lloyd C. Stark	1937 - 1941	Democratic
Forrest C. Donnell	1941 - 1945	Republican
Phil M. Donnelly	1945 - 1949	Democratic
Forrest Smith	1949 - 1953	Democratic
Phil M. Donnelly	1953 - 1957	Democratic
James T. Blair, Jr.	1857 - 1961	Democratic
John M. Dalton	1961 - 1965	Democratic
Warren E. Hearnes	1965 - 1973	Democratic
Christopher S. Bond	1973 - 1977	Republican
Joseph P. Teasdale	1977 - 1981	Democratic
Christopher S. Bond	1981 - 1985	Republican
John Ashcroft	1985 - 1993	Republican
Mel Carnahan	1993 - 2000	Democratic
Roger B. Wilson	2000 - 2001	Democratic
[to come]	2001 -	[to come]

Glossary

A

abolitionist a person who wanted to do away with slavery (4)

academy a type of school established after the Civil War to educate girls (5)

agriculture farming (2)

ally a person, group, or country that helps or cooperates with another (3)

amendment an official addition to a document (6)

American Revolutionary War the war fought by the American colonies in the 1770s to gain their independence from Great Britain (3)

ancestor a person from whom one is descended (2)

appeal to ask that a higher court take another look at a case or lawsuit (10)

artifacts the everyday things that people made and used, such as tools and pottery; clues to how people lived (1)

assembly line a way of putting large numbers of cars —or other products—together; the product is on a moving belt and people and robots add the parts to the product as it moves past them (7)

B

barge a large flat-bottomed boat used on rivers and canals to carry goods (7)

bill a suggested law (10)

blues a type of music that is based on black folk music (6)

boom town a town that grew up quickly, usually because some mineral was found nearby (11)

border to touch or lay alongside something; an imaginary line that separates one state from another (1)

border state a slave state, such as Missouri, that stayed in the Union during the Civil War; the border states lay between the North and the South (4)

boycott a kind of protest where people refuse to do business with a certain store, restaurant, or company (8)

bushwhacker a member of a small group of rebels during the Civil War that raided small towns and farms for supplies (4)

busing a method of integrating schools where African-American students were sent by bus to all-white schools and white students were sent by bus to all-black schools (8)

C

capital the city where the seat of government is located (3)

Capitol the building where the General Assembly meets and the governor's office is located (10)

cash crop a crop that is raised to be sold for a profit; cotton and tobacco were usually cash crops (4)

century a period of 100 years (1)

Civil Rights Acts laws passed in 1964 and 1965 that barred discrimination based on race, creed, or color (8)

climate the weather conditions for a place over a long period of time (2)

commission a type of county government that is made up of two commissioners elected from districts and one commissioner who represents the whole county; can decide how to spend county money but cannot pass laws (10)

committee a group of representatives, senators, or both who meet to study a bill (10)

compromise a way to settle a disagreement in which each side gives way a little in its demands (4)

Confederate States of America the government set up by the southern states that seceded from the Union in the 1860s (4)

conservation preserving our resources by only using what we need (9)

constituents the people who live in a legislator's district (10)

constitution a document that sets out the rules under which a government, or any organization, will operate (4)

continent a large body of land on earth, such as North America (2)

cooperative a group whose members share profits and costs (6)

council a gathering of people, such as the men in an

Indian tribe, where important decisions are made (3); a type of local government where the city or county is divided into districts and a council member is elected from each district (10)

country a nation or area of land with its own government, such as the United States (2)

county a subdivision or smaller part of a state (2)

credit the ability to buy something now and pay for it later (6)

culture the way of life of a group of people; it includes all of their beliefs, customs, activities, and possessions (3)

D

dam a barrier built across a river to control river current or water level (7)

debt money owed to others (6)

decade a period of 10 years (5)

denomination a particular religious group, such as Methodist or Catholic (2)

depression a hard time in the economy when sales and prices of goods decrease, businesses slow down or close, banks fail, and people lose their jobs (6)

diary a personal record of the things that happen to an individual or a personal record of feelings and beliefs (1)

dictator a ruler who has complete control and does not let the people have a say in what the government does (6)

discrimination unequal and unfair treatment that denies people their rights because of their race, sex, religion, or other reason (8)

document a written record of something, such as a newspaper, a legal record, a diary, a family record, or a letter (1)

drought a long period without rain (12)

E

economy the whole system of growing, making, selling, buying, and using goods and services (4)

elevation the distance or height above sea level (2)

e-mail a way of sending messages electronically through the use of a computer; messages arrive almost immediately after they are sent (7)

epidemic a disease that spreads quickly to many other people in the community (5)

equator an imaginary dividing line that lies halfway between the North Pole and the South Pole; divides Earth into northern and southern hemispheres (2)

erosion the washing away of the soil by water or the blowing away of the soil by the wind (9)

evict to force a person off the land or out of a home (8)

executive branch the branch of government that is charged with making sure the state's laws are obeyed; the governor is the head of the executive branch (10)

exodus departure (8)

expedition a journey for a specific purpose, such as exploration (3)

F

flatboat a raft with sides used on the rivers; men on the flatboat pushed a long pole against the river bottom to move the boat (4)

fossil the remains of a creature that have hardened into rock (2)

free state a state that did not permit slavery (4)

Freedmen's Bureau an organization founded by the federal government in 1865 to provide former slaves with food, clothing, medical care, education, and other help (8)

French and Indian War the war fought between France and Great Britain in America in the 1760s; France lost the war and had to give all its land in Canada and east of the Mississippi River to Great Britain (3)

frontier the area just on the edge of a settled area (4)

G

General Assembly the name of Missouri's state legislature (10)

geology the study of the features and structure of the land (3)

geographer a person who studies Earth and the places and people on it (2)

geography the study of Earth, the places and peoples of Earth, and how they relate to one another (2)

Glacial Plains the northern part of the state from the Iowa border to the Missouri River (2)

glaciers large sheets of ice that, during the Ice Age, stretched from the North Pole south to where the Missouri River is today (2)

governor the head of the executive branch of the state government; oversees the operation of the state (10)

H

headwaters streams that flow from the source of a river (3)

hemisphere half of a sphere (2)

historian a person who finds out about the past (1)

historic period the time of written records (3)

historic site a place where an important event in the past took place (1)

history the story of people—who they were, when they lived, where they lived, what their lives were like, and so on (1)

House of Representatives one house of Missouri's General Assembly (10)

hunter/gatherers the early peoples who came to North America and both hunted and gathered their food (3)

I

igneous rock rock that is formed when magma (the liquid rock inside Earth) cools (2)

immigrant one who comes into a country to settle there (2)

independent to be free from the rule of another (3)

integration the process of bringing different groups (races) into society as equals (8)

interstate highway a highway that connects several states (7)

interview to ask questions of a person (1)

irrigate to bring water to crops to help them grow (9)

J

Jim Crow laws laws passed after Reconstruction that prevented blacks from using the same buildings and public services as whites (8)

judicial branch the branch of state government that is made up of the courts and judges (10)

K

keelboat a boat used on the rivers that had a bow and a keel—a strong piece of wood or metal that ran along the bottom of the boat; men on the keelboat pushed a long pole against the river bottom to move the boat (4)

Ku Klux Klan an organization formed by former Confederate soldiers after the Civil War that later became a racist organization opposed to blacks, Catholics, Jews, and others (8)

L

labor union a organization of workers formed to improve the wages and working conditions of the workers (8)

legislative branch the branch of government that makes the laws for the state (10)

locks a method of getting around a dam on a river; gates at either end of the lock allow water in and out to raise or lower the water level so the boat can move upstream or downstream (7)

lumberjack one whose job it is to cut and prepare timber (5)

lynching mob murder, usually by hanging (8)

M

maize the Indian word for corn (3)

manufacturing taking a natural resource (such as wood) and turning it into a product (such as furniture) (5)

map a drawing of an area that shows important features such as roads, towns, rivers, and boundaries (1)

media means of communication such as television, radio, newspapers, and books (1)

militia an army made up of ordinary citizens (3)

minerals natural resources that are found in the ground (9)

missionary one who is sent to do religious work in another country (3)

Missouri Compromise a compromise in Congress that allowed Missouri to enter the Union as a slave state and Maine to enter as a free state; it also banned any slave states north of a line even with Missouri's southern border (4)

municipality a village, town, or city (10)

mural a large painting on a wall (11)

museum a place where items from the past—such as documents, clothes, and furniture—are on display (1)

N

natural resource something found in nature and used by people (9)

network computers that are linked together (7)

neutral to stay out of fighting or to not take sides in a disagreement (6)

New Deal the programs started by President Franklin Roosevelt to help people and the economy recover from the Great Depression (6)

nomad one who moves around and does not live in one place for long (3)

O

observation a careful look at what is around you (1)

oral history a story of the past that has been told by one person to another (1)

Ozark Highlands a region that covers most of the southern and southeastern part of the state (2)

P

petroglyphs rock carvings left by prehistoric peoples (11)

pollution substances that make our air and water dirty and unsafe (9)

Populists members of the People's party formed in the late 1800s to help farmers (6)

precipitation rain and snow (2)

prime meridian an imaginary dividing line that runs from the North Pole through Greenwich, England, to the South Pole; divides Earth into eastern and western hemispheres (2)

professional a person who went to college to learn how to do his or her job (7)

Progressives people who believed that government should help make life better for everyone (6)

prohibition laws that made the manufacture, sale, and use of alcoholic beverages illegal (6)

publish to print for the general public (7)

Q

quarry a large hole in the ground or in the hillside from which minerals are mined (9)

R

racism the belief that a person's own race is better than all others (8)

Radicals the political party that opposed slavery and thought those who had supported slavery should be punished (5)

ragtime a type of music that is a blend of Negro spirituals, march music, and popular tunes played with a quick beat, usually on a piano (6)

ratify to approve something, such as a legislation (6)

ration to limit the use of something (6)

raw materials any materials that are processed to make another product (5)

Reconstruction the period immediately after the Civil War when Missouri had to rebuild its homes and farms, cities and towns, roads, and government (5)

recycle to reuse, especially to collect used materials and make them into new products (6)

region an area of Earth that has many common features (2)

repeal to cancel something, such as a law (4)

reservation an area of land set aside for the Indians, generally in the western states (2)

retail worker a person who works in a store (7)

riot a violent, public disorder (8)

rotate to plant a different crop every year in a particular field so as not to wear out the soil (9)

rural used to describe an area outside a city (2)

S

secede to leave the Union (4)

sedimentary rock rock formed when the skeletons of sea creatures sink to the bottom and are crushed together over millions of years (2)

segregate to separate by race (5)

Senate one house of Missouri's General Assembly (10)

service worker one whose job it is to do something for others for a fee (7)

Sharecroppers Rebellion a march by sharecroppers and their families along highways in the Bootheel, organized by Reverend Owen Whitfield, to demonstrate the conditions faced by the sharecroppers (8)

sit-in a kind of protest where people go into a building and refuse to leave until they are served or forced to leave (8)

skirmish a small clash or minor battle (4)

slave a person who is considered to be the property of another and who is forced to work for that person (2)

slave state a state that permitted slavery (4)

slum a poor, dirty, crowded section of a city (8)

software instructions that tell a computer what to do (7)

Southeast Lowlands the region in the southeast corner of the state; includes the Bootheel (2)

sphere an object that has a round shape (2)

stagecoach a large wagon that had a roof and was pulled by several horses; used to carry people and the mail in the 1800s (4)

state a subdivision of the United States (2)

states' rights a belief that the rights of the individual states are more important than the rights of the federal government (4)

stock shares of ownership in a company (6)

stockyard a place where cattle, pigs, horses, and mules are bought and sold (5)

streetcar an electric-powered form of transportation similar to a railroad that ran along rails laid in the street (7)

strip mining open-pit mining where large shovels remove the top layer of the soil to get to the minerals that lie just below the surface (9)

suffrage the right to vote (8)

symbol one thing that stands for another thing (1)

T

taxes the money people and businesses pay to the government for the services the government provides (6)

technology applying science to solve problems or improve procedures in our everyday lives (7)

tenant farmer a farmer who raised crops on land that belonged to someone else in return for a place to live, seed for the crops, and either a wage or a part of the money earned from selling the crop; also known as a sharecropper (5)

tenement a building similar to an apartment building but that housed only three or four families (5)

terminal a dock where coal, grain, chemicals, fuels, or other cargoes are loaded onto or unloaded from barges (7)

test oath a requirement of the 1865 constitution; in order to vote or hold office Missourians had to swear that they had never supported the Confederacy (5)

tornado a violent windstorm of strong, whirling winds that can knock down houses and uproot trees (2)

tourism an industry that depends on people visiting an area for fun (7)

treaty a formal agreement between two or more sides (3)

tribe a group of people who have common ancestors and who share a name, language, and way of living (3)

U

urban used to describe a town or city (2)

V

vaccine a substance that protects us from diseases (7)

veterinarian a doctor who cares for and treats farm animals and pets (7)

veto the governor's power to refuse to approve a bill (10)

village a municipality with fewer than 500 people (10)

W

weather the day-to-day changes in the temperature and precipitation (2)

Western Plains the southwestern region of the state (2)

wigwam a shelter used by early Native Americans made from poles covered with reed mats (3)

written history a record of the past that has been put down on paper (1)

Index

The purpose of the index is to help you locate information quickly. The index contains references not only to text, but also to illustrations and maps. A page number with an **m** before it indicates a map. A page number with a **p** before it indicates a photograph, painting, or other type of illustration.

A

abolitionists, 90
academy, 104, 106
Adair County, **m**13, 259
Adams, Betty, 184
African Americans, 38, 155, 168, 175, 178-179
  and civil rights movement, 180, 184
  after the Civil War, 102-103, 104, 168, 170, 172
  and discrimination, 170, 173
  and Great Depression, 177-178
  Jim Crow laws, 172-173
  and Ku Klux Klan, 176-177
  and segregation, 174
  and voting, 170
  See also blacks, slaves.
Africans, 37
agriculture, 24, 56, 113
  after the Civil War, 102, 113
  early, 69-73
  equipment for, 125, 128, 161, 162
  modern, 161-164
  and tenant farmers, 102, 103, 177
  See also farmers, farming.
aircraft, 149-150, 251
ally, 59
amendment, 131, 206
American Indians, 36, 46, 63, 64, 88, 220
  clothing, 52
  culture, 48-53

food, 49-50
games, 44
government, 50
Hopewell Indians, 43
hunter/gatherers, 42
Mississippi Indians, 45
language groups, 46
mounds, 43, 45, **p**45
nomads, 42
prehistoric, 40
religion, 50-51
shelter, 48, 50
storytelling, 52
Trail of Tears, 218-219
tribes, 46, **m**48
Woodland Indians, 42-43
American Revolutionary War, 60
Amish, 229, **p**229
ancestors, 36, 46
Anderson, "Bloody Bill," 96, **p**96, 97
Andrew County, **m**13, 259
Angelou, Maya, 238, **p**238-239
Anheuser-Busch, **p**112, **p**160, 164
animals, 34-35, 161-162, 163
antislavery movement, 90-91
appeal, 207
Appleton City, 161
Arrow Rock, **p**5, 9, 82, 108, **p**226, 227
artifacts, 2
assembly line, 146
Atchinson County, **m**13, 259
Atchinson, David Rice, 215
Audrain County, **m**13, 259
Augusta, 164
automobiles, 123-125, 146, 148-149

B

Bagnell Dam, 31, 195, **p**195, 230
Baker, Josephine, 240, **p**240
barge, 152-153, **p**152

Barnett, Marguerite Rose, 184
Barry County, **m**13, 259
Barton County, **m**13, 259
baseball, 106, 137, 236
Basie, Count, 240-242, **p**243
Bates County, **m**13, 259
Bell, Cool Papa, 236
Benton County, **m**13, 259
Benton, Thomas Hart (artist), 226, 242, **p**243
  paintings and drawings, **p**37, **p**138-139, **p**178-179, **p**242-243
Benton, Thomas Hart (politician), 242, **p**242
Bering land bridge, 40, **m**40
Bernie, 161
Berra, Yogi, 256
Berry, Chuck, 256
Bethel, 225
Big Spring, 223
bill, 206
Bingham, George Caleb, 108, **p**108, 256
  paintings and drawings of, **p**78-79, **p**202-203
biotech research, 163
birds, 34, 35, 224, 228
Black River, 28, 31, 222, **p**222
blacks, 155
  and education, 90, 104, 171
  free, 90
  life after slavery, 102-103, 170
  See also African Americans, slaves.
Bloomfield, 161
Blow, Susan, 246
Blue Springs, 235
blues, 136-137
Bluford, Lucille, 181, 246-247, **p**247
Boeing Corporation, 150, 167
Bollinger County, **m**13, 259
Bollinger Mill, **p**2, 218
Bonne Terre, 112, 221
boom town, 232

Boone County, **m**13, 106, 210, 259
Boone, Daniel, 59, 247, **p**247, 248
Boone, Nathaniel, 247, 248
Boonville, 200, 227
Bootheel, 13, 22, 113, 216, 217
border, 6
border state, 93
Bourbon, 161
Bourgmont, Etienne Veniard de, 56
Bowling Green, 224
boycott, 182
Bradley, Bill, 256
Bradley, General Omar, 140
Braggadocio, 216
branches of government,
    executive, 202, 204
    judicial, 207
    legislative, 205-206
Branson, 150, 230
bridges, **p**101, 110, 218, **p**218
Brown, William Wells, 256
Browns, St. Louis, 137
Brunswick, 29, 56, 161, 228
Buchanan County, **m**13, 210, 215,
    259
Burfordville, **p**2
Bull Shoals Lake, 31
Bumbry, Grace, 256
Bushwacker Museum, 199
bushwackers, 94, 95, 96-97
business, 74, 75, 76, 77, 124-125,
    149-150, 163. *See also* economy.
busing, 181
Butler County, **m**13, 259

C
Caldwell County, **m**13, 259
California, 163
Callaway County, **m**13, 69, 259
Calloway, DeVerne Lee, 184, **p**184
Camden County, **m**13, 259
Camdenton, 31
Campbell, 216
Canton, 154
Cape Girardeau, 104, 117, 150,
    152, 218
Cape Girardeau County, **m**13, 259

capital, 59, 68-69
Capitol, State, **p**iv-v, 202, 208-209,
    p208, **p**209
Cardinals, St. Louis, 137
Cardwell, 22
Carnahan, Mel, **p**204
Carnegie, Dale, 256
Carroll County, **m**13, 259
Carson, Kit, 256, **p**256
Carter County, **m**13, 223, 259
Carthage, 112
Carver, George Washington, 248-
    249, **p**249
cash crop, 73
Cass County, **m**13, 259
caves, 18, 42
Cedar County, **m**13, 259
Central Missouri State University,
    104, 233
Centralia, 96-97, 161
century, 4
Charbonneau, Toussaint, 61
Chariton County, **m**13, 250
Chariton River, 29
child labor, 118, 128
Chillicothe, 229
Chopin, Kate O'Flaherty, 256
Chouteau, Auguste, 59, **p**59 , 65
Chouteau, Therese, 59
Christian County, **m**13, 259
Churchill, Winston, 225
circuit courts, 206
cities, 117-119, 128, 212-213
Citizens Liberty League, 176
Civil Rights Acts, 182
civil rights movement, 180-184,
    p182, 247
Civil War,
    causes of, 68, 90-91
    end of, 98
    fighting in Missouri, 93-95, **m**93
    life of soldiers, 95-96
    and Reconstruction, 101
Clark County, **m**13, 192, 200, 259
Clark, William, 61-62, **p**61
Clarksville, 154, 224
clay, 112

Clay County, **m**13, 210, 259
Clay, William, 184
Claycomo, 148
Clearwater Lake, 31
Clemens, Samuel, 109, **p**109, 224,
    254-255, **p**254
climate, 26-27
Clinton, 233
Clinton County, **m**13, 259
coal, 112, 192, 228
Cole County, **m**13, 69, 259
colleges, 104, 113
Columbia, 150, 198, 200, 226
Columbus, Christopher, 46
commission form of government,
    212
committee, 206
communication, 154-156
compromise, 68
computers, 156
Conception, 237
Confederate States of America, 91,
    93. *See also* Civil War.
conservation, 194, 196, 197
constituents, 206
constitution, state, 68, 101, 102, 104
continent, 11
Cooper County, m13, 259
cooperatives, farmers', 128
corn cob pipes, 114, 115
cotton, 113, 216, **p**216
council, 50, 210
counties, 13, **m**13, 210, 212, 259-
    262
countries, 11
county,13, **m**13
    fairs, 106, 113
    government, 210, 213
court of appeals, 207
court system, state, 207
Crawford County, **m**13, 260
credit, buying on, 132
Cronkite, Walter, 256, **p**257
crops, 24, 113, 161
    cash, 73
    irrigation of, 193
    rotation of, 190

Crow, Sheryl, 256
Crowder, Gen. Enoch H., 201
Crowley's Ridge, 216-217
cultural activities, 106, 108-109
culture, Indian, 48-63
Current River, 28, 223

D
Dade County, **m**13, 260
Dallas County, **m**13, 260
dams, 153-154, **p**154
Daviess County, **m**13, 260
Dean, Dizzy and Paul, 137, **p**137
debt, 132
decade, 108
Defiance, 221, 247
DeKalb County, **m**13, 260
denomination, 38
Dent County, **m**13, 260
depression, 134. *See also* Great
  Depression.
DeSoto, 220
Dexter, 161
Diamond, 248
diary, 5
dictators, 138
discrimination, 170, 184, 186
Disney, Walt, 228, 250, **p**250
documents, 2
Douglas County, **m**13, 260
drought, 255
Duchesne, Rose Philippine, 250-
  251, **p**251
Dunklin County, **m**13, 22, 260

E
Eads Bridge, 110-111, **p**110
earthquakes, 21, 218
eastern bluebird, 258
economy, 69, 101
  after the Civil War, 110-113
  early, 69, 74-77
  and Great Depression, 132, 134
  and manufacturing, 77, 160-161
  and slavery, 88-89
  and tourism, 165-166
education, 103, 104, 105, 165

for blacks, 104, 171, 172, 174
  and integration, 180-181
  and the Progressives, 128
See also schools.
electric power, 117, 193, 195
Elephant Rocks State Park, **p**10-11,
  223
elevation, 20, 27
Eleven Point River, 223
Eliot, T. S., **p**136, 137
Elmer, 228
e-mail, 156
energy, alternative, 195. *See also*
  electric power.
entertainment, 106, 136-137
epidemic, 119
equator, 11, 27
erosion, 190
Ethel, 228
European explorers, 46
evict, 178
Excelsior Springs, 163, 234
executive branch of government,
  202, 204
exodus, 175
expedition, 54
expedition, Lewis & Clark, 61-62
explorers, European, 54-55

F
factories, 77, 132, 146, 148, 160,
  161
farmers, 69, 85, 117, 132, 134, 135,
  175
  cooperatives for, 128
  tenant, 102, 103, 135, 177
farming, 17, 20, 24, 113, 162-163,
  193. *See also* agriculture.
Fenton, 148
festivals, 200, 223, 225, 228
Field, Eugene, 109, **p**109
fireclay, 192
fish, 35
flag, state, 6, **p**6, 7
flatboat, 79
Fletcher, 221
floods, 27

Florida, 225, 254
food, American Indian, 49-50
forests, 191, 196, 223
Fort Davidson, 97, **p**97, 222
Fort Howard, 63, 64
Fort Orleans, 56, 228
Fort Osage, **p**x-1, 63, **p**63, 64, **p**64,
  234, **p**234
fossils, 18
Fox Indians, 46
Foxx, Redd, 256
France, 54
  fur trappers from, 55-56
  and Louisiana Purchase, 60-61,
    m61
  settlers from, 56, 58
Frankenstein, 223
Franklin, 82, 155, 227
Franklin County, **m**13, 210, 260
free blacks, 90
free state, 66
Freeburg, 223
Freedmen's Bureau, 170, 171
French and Indian War, 59
French settlers, 37
frontier, 74
Fulton, 112, 225, 253
fur trading, 69
fur trappers, 37, 55-56

G
Gaines, Lloyd, 180-181
Gant, Mary, 185, **p**185
Gasconade County, **m**13, 260
Gasconade River, 28, 79, 83
Gateway Arch, **p**ii-iii, 199, **p**199,
  220, **p**220
General Assembly, 176, 204, 205,
  206, 212, 226
Gentry County, **m**13, 260
geographer, 14
geography, 14-25
geology, 18, 20, 62
German immigrants, 37-38, 90,
  114, 221, 223
Giles, Gwen, 184
Glacial Plains, 16-17, **p**16, **p**17,

224-229
glaciers, 16
Glasgow, 29, 79, 110, 121, 227
Godwin, Dr. Linda, 150, p150
government,
    American Indian, 50
    local, 210-213
    state, 68, 69, 101, 202-209
governor, 202, 204, 263-264
Governor's Mansion, 201, p204
Graham Cave State Park, p40-41, 42
Grand River, 29, 56, 228
Graniteville, 221
Great Britain, 37, 59, 60, 63
Great Depression, 131-134, 138, 177-178
Great Plains, 24
Green City, 228
Green Top, 228
Greencastle, 228
Greene County, m13, 210, 260
Greensburg, 228
Gregory, Dick, 256, p256
Grundy County, m13, 260

H
Hall, Joyce C., 158, p158
Hallmark Cards, 156, 158-159
Hamilton, 228
Hammond, Blaine, 150
Handy, W. C, 137
Hannibal, 31, 85, 110, 112, 117, 224, p224, 254
Hannibal and St. Joseph Railroad, 83
Harmon, Clarence, 184
Harrison County, m13, 260
Hazelwood, 148
headwaters, 62
health care, 119, 157, 160
hemispheres, 11, m12
Hematite, 221
Henry County, m13, 260
Hermann, 28, 198, 223, p223
Hermitage, 161
Hickory County, m13, 260
Higginsville, 233

highways, 149
hillbillies, 230, 231
historian, 2
historic period, 46
historic site, 4, 5, 198-199
history, 2, 4, 5, 198
honeybee, 6, p6
Holt County, m13, 260
Hopewell Indians, 43
House of Representatives, state, 205, 206, 209
houses, early, 58, p71
Howard County, m13, 260
Howell County, m13, 260
Hubble, Edwin, 256
Hughes, James Langston, 256, p257
hunter/gatherers, 42

I
Iberia, 161
Ice Age, 16
igneous rock, 20
Illinois Indians, 46
immigrants, 37, 38, 90, 119, 155, 186, 223, 224
Imperial, 198
income tax, 213-214
independence, 60
Independence, 82, 234-235
Indians, 46. *See also* American Indians.
integration, 181
Internet, 156
interstate highways, m148, 149
interview, 4
Iowa Indians, 46
iron, 221
Iron County, m13, 191, 201, 260
Ironton, 192, 221
irrigate, 193

J
Jacks Fork River, 223
Jackson, 161
Jackson, Claiborne, 93
Jackson County, m13, 210, 260
Jaeger, Herman, 256

James brothers, 96, 102, p102, 215
Jamesport, 228, 229
Jasper County, m13, 192, 260
Jefferson City, 28, 69, p69, 83, 93, 161, 182, 202, 208, 226, p226
Jefferson County, m13, 210, 260
Jim Crow laws, 173, 182
Johnson County, m13, 260
Johnson Shut-Ins State Park, 222, p222
Jolliet, Louis, 54-55
Joplin, 27, 111, 112, 161, 232
Joplin, Scott, 136, p136, 199
judicial branch of government, 207

K
Kahoka, 200
Kansa Indians, 46
Kansas, 91
Kansas City, 28, 83, 85, 110, 112, 117, 146, 150, 151, 152, 156, 158, 159, 163, 175, 183, 235-236
Kansas City Call, 155, 247
Kansas City Monarchs, 137
Katy Trail, 198, 220, 227
keelboat, 79
Kennett, 199
kindergarten, 246
King, Dr. Martin Luther, Jr., 182, p182, 183
King City, 237
Kirksville, 27, 104, 160, 228
Knox County, m13, 260
Ku Klux Klan, 176-177

L
labor union, 174
Laclede County, m13, 260
Laclede, Pierre, 59, p59
Lafayette County, m13, 260
Lake of the Ozarks, 31, p31, 35, 230
Lake Wappapello, 31
lakes, m30. *See also* specific lakes.
Lamar, 142, 199, 233
land bridge, 40, m40
Lawrence County, m13, 261
laws, making, 206

lead, 55, 112, 191, 223
Leadington, 221
Lear, William P., 150
Lebanon, 198, 230
legislative branch of government, 205-206
legislators, 205
legislature, state, 205
Lesterville, 222
Lewis County, m13, 261
Lewis, Meriwether, 61-62, 63
Lexington, 79, 94, 233
Liberty, 234
Licking, 161
lieutenant governor, 202, 204
light rail lines, 151
limestone, 112, 192, 208
Lincoln, Abraham, 91, p91
Lincoln County, m13, 261
Lincoln University, 104, 172, 181, 247
Lindbergh, Charles A., 251-252, p252
Linn, 161
Linn County, m13, 261
literature, 136
Little River, p23
Livingston County, m13, 261
local government, 210, 212-214
locks, 153
Locust Creek, 228
Louisiana, 55, 59, 63
    Purchase, 60-61, m61
    Territory of, 62-63
Louisiana (city), 224
Louisiana Purchase Centennial
    Exposition, 126-127, p126, p127
lumber industry, 20, 23, 113
lumberjacks, 113
lynching, 171, 174, 177

M
Macon, 228
Macon County, m13, 261
Madison County, m13, 261
maize, 49
Malone, Annie, 256

Mansfield, 230, 255
manufacturing, 77, 110, 112, 160-161
maps, 7, m8, m12, m13, m14, m27, m30, m40, m48, m61, m68, m82, m86, m91, m93, m148, m192
Marceline, 85, 228, 250
Maries County, m13, 223, 261
Mark Twain Lake, 31, p31, 225
Mark Twain National Forest, 223
Marquette, Pere Jacques, 54-55
Marshall, 163, 229
Maryville, 128, 237
McBride, Mary Margaret, 256
McDonald County, m13, 261
McDonnell-Douglas Aircraft
    Corporation, 149-150
McDonnell, James S., 149
McGwire, Mark, 256
McNeal, Theodore D., 184, p184
McRae, Hal, 184
Meachum, John Berry, 90
media, 5
Meramec River, 20, 28, p29
Mercer County, m13, 261
Mexico, 112, 225
Miami, 229
militia, 64, 93
Miller County, m13, 261
Mina Sauk Falls, 39, 222
Mine LaMotte, 55, 219
Mineral Fork, p19
Mineral Point, 221
minerals, 20, 55, 188, 190
mines, 20, 24, 112, 221
mining, 221-222, 228
missionary, 55
Mississippi County, m13, 261
Mississippi Indians, 45
Mississippi River, 28, p28, 35, 42, 54, 60, 79, 90, 153-154, 254, 255
Missouri Compromise, 68, m68
Missouri Department of Conservation, 196
Missouri Equal Rights League, 171, 172

Missouri Farmers Association, 128
Missouri Gazette, 155
Missouri Human Rights Commission, 184, 247
Missouri Indians, 36, p36, 46, 56
Missouri Intelligencer and Boon's Lick Advertiser, 155
Missouri River, 14, p14-15, 28, 42, 55, 56, 62, 79, 108, 121, 154, 221, 229, 236
Missouri Territory, 63, 66
Missouri Town, p72-73, p74, 235, p235
Moberly, 85, 228
Monett, 200
Moniteau County, m13, 261
Monroe City, 31
Monroe County, m13, 261
Montgomery City, 224
Montgomery County, m13, 261
Moore, Marianne, 137
Moore, Walthall, 176
Morgan County, m13, 261
Mormons, 186
motto, state, 8, 202
mounds, Indian, 43, 45, p45
Mountain Grove, 230
Mountain View, 230
municipality, 212
mural, p37, 226, 242, p244-245
museums, 4, p4, 199
music,
    blues, 136-137
    country, 230
    ragtime, 136
    jazz, 241, 242

N
National Association for the
    Advancement of Colored People
    (NAACP), 174
Native Americans, *see* American
    Indians.
natural resources, 110, 188-194
    and conservation, 194
    forests, 191
    minerals, 188, 190, 191-192

and pollution, 191
   soil, 188, 190
   water, 20, 193-194
Neosho, 93
network, 156
neutral, 129
Nevada, 199
New Deal, 134, 135, 177
New Madrid County, **m**13, 261
New Madrid, earthquakes, 21, 218
newspapers, 130, 155, 174
Newton County, **m**13, 261
Nodaway County, **m**13, 261
nomads, 42
Norfolk Lake, 31
Northwest Missouri State University, 128, 237
Novinger, 228

O
observations, 5
ocean, effect on Missouri, 18, 27
O'Fallon, 156
Old Mines, 221
oral history, 2, 4
oral history form, 3
Oregon County, **m**13, 261
Oregon Trail, 81, 82, **m**82
Osage County, **m**13, 223, 261
Osage Indians, 45, 46, 48, 49-52, **p**52, **p**53. *See also* American Indians.
Osage River, 28, 31, 35, 48, 68, 79, 233
Oto Indians, 46
outlaws, 102
Overland Mail, 82-83
Ozark County, **m**13, 261
Ozark Highlands, 18-20, 230, 231
Ozark Mountains, 20, 219

P
Pacific Railroad, 83
Paige, Satchel, 137, 236
Paris, 225
Park Hills, 222
parks, state, 230

Pemiscot County, **m**13, 216, **p**216, 261
Penney, James Cash, 228
people, 36-38
Perkins, Marlin, 256
Perry County, **m**13, 261
Pershing, General John, 130
petroglyphs, **p**44, 45, 220
Pettis County, **m**13, 261
Phelps County, **m**13, 261
Piedmont, 31
Pike County, **m**13, **p**28, 261
Pilot Knob, 222
Pilot Knob, Battle of, 97
pipes, corn cob, 115
plants, 32-33
Platte County, **m**13, 261
political party, 128
Polk County, **m**13, 261
pollution, 191, 192, 194
Pony Express, 86-87, **m**86, 237
Pony Express Museum, **p**86, 199
Poplar Bluff, 31
Populists, 128
prairie, **p**25
precipitation, 27, **m**27
prehistoric peoples,
   Hopewell Indians, 43
   Mississippi Indians, 45
   Woodland Indians, 42-43
Price, Sterling, 96, 97, **p**98, 99
Price, Vincent, 256
prime meridian, 11
professionals, 165
Progressives, 128
prohibition, 131
property tax, 210, 214
Pruitt, Capt. Wendell Oliver, 168, 178
publishing, 155-156
Pulaski County, **m**13, 261
Pulitzer, Joseph, 256
Putnam County, **m**13, 261

Q
Quapaw Indians, 45, 46
quarry, 192

R
racism, 170
Radicals, 101, 104
radio, 135
ragtime, 136
railroads, 81, **m**82, 83, 85, 110-111, 112, 113, 128, 150-151, **p**151
rainfall, 27, **m**27
Ralls County, **m**13, 262
Randolph County, **m**13, 262
rapid transit, 151
ratify, 131
rationing, 138
raw materials, 112
Ray County, **m**13, 262
Reconstruction, 101-102, 170, 172
recreation, 20, 193
recycling, 138-139, 194
re-enactments, 200, **p**200
regions, 14-25, **m**14
religion, 38, 50-51, 55, 108, 229
repeal, 90
Republican party, 91
reservations, 36
resources, 188, 194
retail workers, 165
Revolutionary War, 60
Reynolds County, **m**13, 191, 262
Richards, Richard N., 150
riots, 182
Ripley County, **m**13, 262
rivers, **p**16, 17, 20, 23, 28-29, , **m**30, 31, 110
   dams on, 153
   travel on, 79-80, 152-153
See also specific rivers.
roads, 79, 124, **m**148, 149
Rocheport, 14, 164, 199, 227, **p**227
rock, 18, 20
Rock Port, 237
Rocketdyne Corporation, 150
Rolla, 85, 112
Roman Catholic religion, 38
Roosevelt, Franklin, 134, **p**134
rotation, crop, 190
rural, 36, 123

S

Sac River, 31
Sacajawea, 61
St. Charles, 61, 69, 110, 152, 208, 220, 250
St. Charles County, **m**13, 149, 210, 247, 262
St. Clair County, **m**13, 262
St. Francis River, 22, **p**22, 28, 31
St. Francois County, **m**13, 262
St. Joseph, 82, 86, 112, 150, 163, 199, 237
St. Louis, 13, 28, 45
  after the Civil War, 110, **p**110-111, 111, 112, **p**116-117, 117
  early, 60, 61, 63, **p**80-81, 85
  modern, 146, **p**146-147, 149, 150, 151, 154, 155, 175, 199, 220-221
  settlement of, 59
St. Louis American, 155
St. Louis Argus, 155
St. Louis Browns, 137
St. Louis Cardinals, 137
St. Louis County, **m**13, 149, 210, 220, 262
St. Louis University, 157
St. Louis World's Fair, 126-127, **p**126, **p**127, 145
St. Patrick, 224
Ste. Genevieve, 56, 58, 219-220
Ste. Genevieve County, **m**13, 262
sales tax, 213
Saline County, **m**13, 262
Salisbury, 228
Salt River, **p**16, 31
Santa Fe Trail, 81, 82, **m**82, 227
Sauk Indians, 46
Saverton, 154
schools, 130, 160, 213
  academies, 104, 106
  for blacks, 171, 173
  and integration, 180-181
  kindergarten, 246
  medical, 157
  teachers' colleges, 104, 172
School of Osteopathy, 157, 160

Schuyler County, **m**13, 262
Schwarzer, Franz, 114, **p**114
Scotland County, **m**13, 262
Scott, Dred and Harriet, **p**252, 252-253
Scott County, **m**13, 262
seal, state, 6, 8
secede, 91
Sedalia, 111, 136, 200, 229
sedimentary rock, 18
segregation, 103, 174, 178, 180
Senate, state, 205, 206, 209
service workers, 164, **p**164
settlers, early, 56, 58
Shannon County, **m**13, 262
sharecropper, 177
Sharecroppers' Rebellion, 178, **p**178
Shelby County, **m**13, 262
Shepard, Alan, Jr., 150, **p**150
shut-ins, 222
Sibley, 64, 234
Sikeston, 216
silver, 192
Silver Dollar City, 230
sit-in, 182
skirmish, 98
slave state, 66, 68
slavery, 88-89, 90-91, 101, 102, 252
slaves, 37, 60, 66
  after the Civil War, 170
  living conditions of, 88
  work done by, 70, 88
slums, 174
Smith, Mellcene Thurman, 185, **p**185
Smith, Reginald, 184
software, 156
soil, 17, 188, 190
song, state, 6
Southeast Lowlands, 22-24, 216-223
Southeast Missouri State University, 104, 218
Southern Baptist religion, 38
Southwest Missouri State University, 128, 232, **p**232

soybeans, 161, **p**161
Spain, 59, 60
sphere, 11
Springfield, 83, 110, 111, 112, 128, 150, 232, **p**232
springs, 20, **p**20, 223, 234
stagecoach, 82-83
state, 11
  becoming a, 66, 68
  bordering, 12, **m**12
State Capitol, piv-v, p69, 202, 208-209, **p**208, **p**209, 226
state flag, 6, **p**6, 7
state government, 69, 202-209
  constitution, 68, 101, 102, 104, 202
  executive branch, 202, 204
  judicial branch, 207
  legislative branch, 205-206
  sources of revenue, 213-214
State Highway Patrol, 125
state historic sites, 4-5
State Line, 216
state motto, 8, 202
state parks, 177, **p**196, 198
state seal, 6, 7
state song, 7
statehood, 66, 68
states' rights, 68
steamboats, 79, 80, **p**106, 153, **p**153
Stengel, Casey, 256
Stephens, Helen, 253, **p**253
stock, 132
Stockton Lake, 31
stockyards, 112, 236
Stoddard County, **m**13, 262
Stone County, **m**13, 262
streetcars, 151
strip mining, 192
suffrage, 172, 185
Sullivan County, **m**13, 262
Sullivan, Leonor K., 185
supreme court, 207
Swan Lake National Wildlife Refuge, 228
symbols, state, 6, 7, 258

T

Table Rock Lake, 31
Taney County, **m**13, 262
Tarkio, 237
Taum Sauk Mountain, 20, 222
taxes, 124, 213-214
  property, 210
  for roads, 124
Taylor, 154
teachers' colleges, 104, 172
Teasdale, Sara, 137, **p**137
technology, 154, 161, 163
  communications, 117, 154-156
  computers, 156
  electrical power, 117
  health care, 157, 160
telephones, 117
television, 155
temperature, 26, 27, **m**27
tenant farmers, 102, 135, 177
tenements, 118, **p**118
terminals, river, 153
test oath, 102
Texas County, **m**13, 262
Tibbe, Henry, 115, **p**115
tiff, 192
Tipton, 83, 230
tobacco, 113, 227, 237
tornadoes, 27
tourism, 165-166
trading posts, 55, 59, 74
Trail of Tears State Park, 218
trails, western, 81, 227
transportation, 79, 81, 146
  aircraft, 149-150
  automobiles, 123-125, 146, 148-
    149
  railroads, 81, **m**82, 83, 85, 110-
    111, 150-151, **p**151
  rapid transit, 151
  on the rivers, 79, 152-153, **p**153
  roads, 79, 124, **m**148, 149
  stagecoaches, 82-83
  trails, 81
treaty, 59
trees, 32, 33. 191
tribe, 46. *See also* American Indians,

specific tribes.
Truman, Harry S, 6, 130, **p**130,
  142-143, **p**142, **p**143, 180, 235,
  257
Truman Reservoir, 31
Truman State University, 104
Turner, Debbye, 184
Turner, James Milton, 171, **p**171,
  172
Turner, Sarah Lucille, 185, **p**185
Twain, Mark, 82, 109, **p**109, 224,
  254-255, **p**254

U

Union Star, 237
University of Missouri, 104, **p**104-
  105, 157, 162, 163, 181, 184,
  226, 246
urban areas, 36, 123, 151. *See also*
  cities.
Urban League, 174, 177
U.S.S. *Missouri*, **p**141

V

vaccine, 157
Valles Mines, 221
Van Dyke, Dick, 256
Van Meter State Park, 43
Vandalia, 224
Vernon County, **m**13, 262
veterinarian, 163
veto, 206
village, 210, 212
Viburnum, 223
Viburnum Trend, 191
volcanoes, effect on Missouri, 20,
  22, 24
voting, 102, 171, 172, 185, 213
Voyage of Discovery, 61-62, **m**61,
  220
voyageurs, 55, 56

W

Walker, 233
war, *see* specific wars.
Warren County, **m**13, 262
Warrensburg, 104, 233

Washington, 114
Washington County, **m**13, 262
Washington State Park, 45
Washington University, 157, **p**157
water resources, 193-194, 222-223
  springs, 20
Watkins Woolen Mill, **p**76, **p**77
Wayne County, **m**13, 262
weather, 26, 27
Webster County, **m**13, 262
Wentzville, 148
West Alton, 154
Western Plains, 24-25, 232-237
Westminster College, 225
Weston, 79, 237
Westphalia, 223
Westport, Battle of, 97-98
White River, 31
Whitfield, Owen, 178
wigwam, 48
Wilder, Laura Ingalls, 230. 255,
  p255
Wilson's Creek, Battle of, **p**92-93,
  93-94
Wilson's Creek National Battlefield,
winds, 27
Winfield, 64, 154
women's rights, 185
Woodland Indians, 42-43
workers, 164, **p**164, 165
World War I, 129-131
World War II, 138-141, **p**140, **p**141,
  178-179
World Wide Web, 156
Worth County, **m**13, 262
Wright, Harold Bell, 137
Wright County, **m**13, 262
writers, 109
written history, 2

Y

Young, Hiram, 256

Z

zinc, 192
zithers, 114, **p**114

Acknowledgements

FRONT MATTER: Cover The Saint Louis Art Museum. i Robin McDonald. ii-iii Robin McDonald. iv-v Robin McDonald. vii Robin McDonald. viii Robin McDonald. ix Robin McDonald. **CHAPTER ONE:** x-1 Robin McDonald. 2 Robin McDonald. 4 (both) Robin McDonald. 5 Robin McDonald. 6 Robin McDonald. 7 Robin McDonald. **CHAPTER TWO:** 10-11 Robin McDonald. 14-15 Robin McDonald. 16 Robin McDonald. 16-17 Robin McDonald. 18-19 Robin McDonald. 19 Robin McDonald. 20 Robin McDonald. 21 State Historical Society of Missouri. 22 Robin McDonald. 22-23 Robin McDonald. 24 Robin McDonald. 25 Robin McDonald. 26-27 Robin McDonald. 28 Robin McDonald. 28-29 Robin McDonald. 30 Robin McDonald. 31 (both) Robin McDonald. 32 (all) Robin McDonald. 33 Robin McDonald. 34 (both) Robin McDonald. 35 (both) Robin McDonald. 36 National Museum of American Art/Art Resources. 37 (above) Robin McDonald, (below) Missouri State Archives. 38 Robin McDonald. **CHAPTER THREE:** 40-41 Robin McDonald. 42 Pinson Mounds State Archeological Area, Tennessee. 43 Pinson Mounds State Archeological Area, Tennessee. 44 (above) Pinson Mounds State Archeological Area, Tennessee, (below) Robin McDonald. 45 Robin McDonald. 46-47 National Museum of American Art/Art Resources. 48 Van Meter State Park/Robin McDonald. 49 National Museum of American Art/Art Resources. 50 Oklahoma Historical Society. 51 Newberry Library, Chicago. 52 State Historical Society of Missouri. 53 National Museum of American Art/Art Resources. 54 Corbis/Bettmann. 55 Corbis/Bettmann. 56 Robin McDonald. 56-57 Robin McDonald. 58 (above) Robin McDonald, (below) Wisconsin Historical Society. 59 (both) State Historical Society of Missouri. 60 Robin McDonald. 61 Corbis/Bettmann. 62 (above) Corbis/Bettmann, (below) State Historical Society of Missouri. 63 Robin McDonald. 64 Robin McDonald. **CHAPTER FOUR:** 66 State Historical Society of Missouri. 67 Robin McDonald. 69 State Historical Society of Missouri. 70 North Carolina Department of Archives and History. 70-71 Robin McDonald. 72 (both) Robin McDonald. 72-73 Robin McDonald. 74 Robin McDonald. 74-75 Robin McDonald. 76 (all) Robin McDonald. 76-77 Robin McDonald. 78-79 The Saint Louis Art Museum. 80-81 The Saint Louis Art Museum. 83 State Historical Society of Missouri. 84 Library of Congress. 84-85 State Historical Society of Missouri. 85 Robin McDonald. 86 Robin McDonald. 87 (both) Robin McDonald. 88-89 Corbis/Bettmann. 90 West Virginia State Archives. 91 Library of Congress. 92-93 Library of Congress. 94 *Battles and Leaders of the Civil War.* 95 *Battles and Leaders of the Civil War.* 96 State Historical Society of Missouri. 97 Robin McDonald. 98 Robin McDonald. **CHAPTER FIVE:** 100-101 Robin McDonald. 101 Rockefeller Library, Colonial Williamsburg, VA. 102 Robin McDonald. 102 (above) Library of Congress, (below) Robin McDonald. 103 State Historical Society of Missouri. 104 Robin McDonald. 104-105 Robin McDonald. 106 Louisiana State Museum. 107 (above) State Historical Society of Missouri, (below) Robin McDonald. 108 (left) Robin McDonald, (right) The Saint Louis Art Museum. 109 (both) State Historical Society of Missouri. 110 Robin McDonald. 110-111 State Historical Society of Missouri. 112 Robin McDonald. 113 Robin McDonald. 113 LC. 114 (both) State Historical Society of Missouri. 115 (above) State Historical Society of Missouri, (below) Robin McDonald. 116-117 State Historical Society of Missouri. 118 State Historical Society of Missouri. 119 State Historical Society of Missouri. 120 Robin McDonald. **CHAPTER SIX:** 122-123 State Historical Society of Missouri. 124 State Historical Society of Missouri. 125 State Historical Society of Missouri. 126 State Historical Society of Missouri. 126-127 State Historical Society of Missouri. 127 Robin McDonald. 128 Robin McDonald. 129 State Historical Society of Missouri. 130 (above) Library of Congress, (below) Corbis/Bettmann. 131 State Historical Society of Missouri. 132 Library of Congress. 133 Library of Congress. 134 (above) Library of Congress, (below) Atlanta Historical Society. 135 Library of Congress. 136 (above) Robin McDonald, (below left) Library of Congress, (below left) Corbis/Bettmann. 137 (above) Corbis/Bettmann, (below) State Historical Society of Missouri. 138-139 State Historical Society of Missouri. 140 LC. 140-141 Corbis/Bettmann. 141 (all) Library of Congress. 142 Library of Congress. 143 Corbis/Bettmann. 144 (both) Robin McDonald. **CHAPTER SEVEN:** 146-147 Robin McDonald. 149 Robin McDonald. 150 (both) National Aeronautics and Space Administration. 151 Robin McDonald. 152 Robin McDonald. 153 Robin McDonald. 154 Robin McDonald. 155 Robin McDonald. 156 Robin McDonald. 157 Robin McDonald. 158 State Historical Society of Missouri. 159 Robin McDonald. 160 Robin McDonald. 161 Robin McDonald. 162 Robin McDonald. 163 (both) Robin McDonald. 164 Robin McDonald. 164 Robin McDonald. 165 Robin McDonald. 166 Robin McDonald. **CHAPTER EIGHT:** 168-169 Library of Congress. 170 Library of Congress. 171 State Historical Society of Missouri. 172 State Historical Society of Missouri. 173 Robin McDonald. 174 State Historical Society of Missouri. 175 Corbis/Bettmann. 176 Library of Congress. 177 Robin McDonald. 178 Western Historical Manuscripts Collection, St. Louis. 178-179 State Historical Society of Missouri. 180 State Historical Society of Missouri. 181 State Historical Society of Missouri. 182 (above) Corbis/Bettmann, (below) Atlanta Historical Society. 183 Corbis/Bettmann. 184 (above) State Historical Society of Missouri, (below) Western Historical Manuscripts Collection, St. Louis. 185 (all) State Historical Society of Missouri. 186 Robin McDonald. **CHAPTER NINE:** 188-189 Robin McDonald. 190 Robin McDonald. 191 Robin McDonald. 192 Robin McDonald. 193 Robin McDonald. 194 Robin McDonald. 195 Robin McDonald. 196 Robin McDonald. 197 Mississippi Department of Tourism 198 Robin McDonald. 199 Robin McDonald. 200 Robin McDonald. **CHAPTER TEN:** 202-203 The Saint Louis Art Museum. 204 (left) Office of the Governor, (right) Robin McDonald. 205 Missouri State Archives. 206 Corbis/Bettmann. 207 Robin McDonald. 208 (above) Robin McDonald, (below) Missouri State Archives. 209 (all) Robin McDonald. 210 Robin McDonald. 211 Robin McDonald. 212 Robin McDonald. 213 Robin McDonald. 214 Robin McDonald. **CHAPTER ELEVEN:** 216-217 Robin McDonald. 218 (both) Robin McDonald. 219 Robin McDonald. 220 (both) Robin McDonald. 221 Robin McDonald. 222 Robin McDonald. 223 Robin McDonald. 224 Robin McDonald. 225 Robin McDonald. 226 (both) Robin McDonald. 227 (both) Robin McDonald. 228 Robin McDonald. 229 Robin McDonald. 229 Robin McDonald. 230 Robin McDonald. 231 State Historical Society of Missouri. 232 (both) Robin McDonald. 233 Robin McDonald. 234 Robin McDonald. 235 (both) Robin McDonald. 236 (both) Robin McDonald. 237 Robin McDonald. **CHAPTER TWELVE:** 238-239 Corbis/Bettmann. 240 Corbis/Bettmann. 241 Oklahoma Historical Society. 242 Library of Congress. 243 State Historical Society of Missouri. 244-245 Harry S Truman Library, Independence. 246 State Historical Society of Missouri. 247 (above) State Historical Society of Missouri, (below) Kentucky Historical Society. 248 Robin McDonald. 249 Alabama Department of Archives and History. 250 Corbis/Bettmann. 251 State Historical Society of Missouri. 252 (above) State Historical Society of Missouri, (below) Corbis/Bettmann. 253 Corbis/Bettmann. 254 State Historical Society of Missouri. 255 State Historical Society of Missouri. 256 (above) Library of Congress, (below) Corbis/Bettmann. 257 (both) Corbis/Bettmann.